**For all who seek the truth
beyond church/bible dogma**

SPIRITUALITY

versus

RELIGION

FREEDOM vs CONTROL

Leo Rutherford

Thanks to my many friends who assisted in the creation and compilation of this book.

ISBN: 1461007941
ISBN-13: 9781461007944

Parts of this book previously published as 'Adam & Evil: the God who hates sex, women and human bodies'. (Trafford Pubs 20080)

By the same author:

The View through the Medicine wheel. O-Books 2007

Shamanic Path Workbook. Arima Publications 2001/2006

Principles of Shamanism /Way of shamanism. Harper Collins/ Thorsons 1996/2001

The book of games and warm-ups for group leaders. Gale Centre publications 1994

CHAPTERS LIST

SPIRITUALITY VERSUS RELIGION
Freedom vs Control

Preface – a boy's horrid memories of 'God', 'right living' and growing up into the 'right kind of chap'.

I grew up in a nice, normal British middle-class family who did their best to be normal and nice and do all the 'right things'. This meant that there was a lot of pressure on me to grow up into the 'right sort' of boy (and man) and so I was sent away early to boarding school so that would happen – and because my parents believed it was the 'right thing' to do. The fact that this was blatant abandonment – at the tender age of eight no less – was quite outside the frame of reference of consensus thinking at that time.

Although, many thanks to my parents, I was not given much religion at home, it was always there as an undertone and I got buckets of it at school. Humans had been thrown out of the 'Garden Of Eden' for disobedience by an angry chap called God. This meant obedience was very important in life, especially among children who must obey their 'elders and betters.' At school I was given the full religious indoctrination with prayers every morning and evening, hymns, psalms, sermons and religious teaching, all of which suggested that a human being was born in sin and had to be urgently baptized, confirmed as a Protestant (and definitely not a Catholic!) at the age of 14 or 15; was not good enough for God without a great deal of training and punishment, must be a good little Christian boy; must believe the Bible as the living word of God and must have nothing whatsoever to do with sex and do everything he's told.

Then came puberty and 'public' school. Now to put it as politely as possible, puberty is a challenge. The body grows extra parts, with urges and agendas of their own. Religion teaches that the one thing you should not do is obey any of those urges – at least not until you are safely married anyway, and even then preferably only for procreation. Anything else is sinful, bad or even terrible, and will gain quite appalling retribution from this kind and loving 'God-Chap'.

All of this helped me to have not just low self-esteem but virtually none at all. I was not at all violent, not good at games, and not a bully, so I had none of the usual ways of assuaging the pain of inadequacy or of 'proving myself'. It seemed I must be worthless not just in the eyes of God, but my teachers and fellows also.

Public school – a strange British euphemism for an expensive private boarding school with heavy duty religious overtones coupled with fiendish punishments, where children of the privileged can be taken off their parents' hands for two thirds of the year and taught to be brutal to each other – attempted to keep pupils so busy and harassed that puberty would pass by unnoticed. A dismal failure, of course. One was left simply trying to survive and get through to senior years when it becomes your job to make the new juniors have as rotten a time as you did. (Another task at which I dismally failed, glad to say.)

To put all the boys together, with no girls and little of the feminine gender at all, at the time when they are going through enormous growth into sexual beings, is quite the strangest of ideas. What on earth did the creators of such a boneheaded system expect to happen? The sexual instinct that cannot be expressed as intended sneaks out in other ways – as described in many biographies of those who suffered this mad 'injurecation'. We fool with nature at our peril.

Religious mythology – the way I was taught it.

God is a wonderful father who created the world. He lives in Heaven with his Only Son Jesus, in a wonderful and perfect place somewhere up above where nothing ever goes wrong and there is absolutely no sin or unhappiness. But he has no wife and no daughters.

God is love. But he is also very judgmental and watching to see any of us who commit sins and tally them up against us, so you have to fear God even though he is 'love'.

Good people believe in God and His Only Son Jesus who He sent to save the world.

You have to be christened as soon as you are born because if you are not and you die, your soul will go to purgatory, which is a very nasty place.

Only Christians get to Heaven because they believe in the only right God. Everyone else is mistaken, misguided and needs to be converted to Christianity for the sake of their souls.

Jesus died for our sins so, even if we commit them, as long as we believe in Jesus, we are going to be all right. We must believe Jesus died for us personally and only if we believe in him fervently will God absolve us of our sins. When we are about to die, we must get ablution (Okay - Freudian slip. In those days, that's how it sounded to me) of our sins, so even if we've committed lots of sins, we'll still be all right.

God is a nice, old, white man with a long white beard, and Jesus is a nice, young, white man (not a trace of Jewishness!) with deep blue eyes, a dark beard and a comforting smile.

Women are less than men in the eyes of God and religion is more a man's thing. Monks are mainly men, saints are mainly men but some women do manage to be godly, especially nuns and unmarried women who never have sex.

Hell is a bad place down below and if you don't want to go there, you must keep trying to be godly by looking up towards heaven. And you must try not to think about, let alone touch, that place down there between your legs because it will take you straight to hell.

Sex is bad and good Christian people do it as little as possible. All proper, godly people do not indulge in sex or sensuality because it is ungodly.

Jesus was born of a virginal mother which is the ideal way to be born. All Christian women are virgins on their wedding day and all Christian married couples only commit sex when they want to have children because to do it for any other purpose is a sin.

Enjoying sex for its own sake is a sin.

Thinking about sex is a sin.

Making yourself look sexy is a temptation to sin.

Sex before marriage is a big sin.

Masturbation is a very big sin.

Homosexuality is a very, very big sin.

Fantasizing about sex is a nasty, big, evil rotten sin.

Jesus never did any of it whatsoever and nor should you (or me) and if you do, you are bad in the eyes of God and will be punished until you stop and probably a lot longer. And if you masturbate, you'll go blind.

Today that might sound absurd and ridiculous but that's the gist of what they taught me. A tight constraining straight-jacket for a boy becoming a teenager and struggling to understand and cope with enormous, powerful and puzzling bodily energies. And with no one at all to talk to, never mind get any sensible guidance from. Amazing when you think about it. This means that any good Christian boy, however good he tries to be, becomes a monstrous sinner in the eyes and ears of the 'God-Chap' as soon as puberty hits. I mean how many adolescent boys don't masturbate or have some sort of sexual release for some (or all) of the time in those years – only the very low drive ones, and even then ….

What a great set up to make all normal boys – and girls too – feel appallingly guilty and inadequate for this ghastly tyrant God-Chap. And therefore to live in denial of their true nature and to fight inwardly against themselves. That is what happened to me. I became a raging war against my own nature as I struggled to become someone different, someone who was acceptable to God, to my parents, teachers and 'elders and betters.' Someone who fitted in with how society presented itself (little did I know it was not at all how is actually was) and with what was considered 'right and proper'.

At the age of nineteen when I felt like a totally lost soul, guilty just for being alive, isolated in the extreme, I somehow ended up at a Billy Graham Evangelical meeting, at the end of which, my legs carried me to the front to 'accept Jesus as my savior'. I then found myself being taught by a rather extreme Christian group who abstained from all sorts of things, read only the Bible, and whose women didn't wear make-up. I was sort of impressed for a bit until I found out, under all the piety, they were just as mean-spirited and bitchy as everyone else. That wonder cure lasted three weeks and I was glad to get back to a more ordinary, less pinched level of madness. I joined the Church of England as the girls were infinitely better looking.

Fortunately, I never really did deeply believe it all. I felt I lived amongst mad people in a mad world and that there must be – somewhere over a very distant rainbow indeed – another way, another world, and people with open hearts who spoke their truth. I gave up on religion and focused on engineering. I felt that machines don't lie, they don't try to make you believe impossible things, they don't set you against yourself, they are not devious, they are just what they are. And one can get skilled at making them work for which I had a natural instinct.

In my thirties I studied once a week in Liverpool with a wonderful yoga teacher, Ken Ratcliffe (International Hermeneutic Society), and for the first time, heard a philosophy that made sense. However, it took a massive mid-life crisis to get me to stop my whole life and start over again. I found I had been right all along – I really had lived in a mad world but now I was no longer alone and isolated. There were others who felt similarly and I received much sensible guidance, therapy and teaching that opened up for me a path to self knowledge and a sense of the deeper meaning of life. This led me to the ways of the ancients, our ancestors who lived before the time of male-domination and all-male 'gods.' Before the time when 'God' went wrong....

We are now seeing the fruits of this collective madness all around us in the serious pollution of the earth and her atmosphere, the over-consumption of her resources, the scandals of the no-so celibate priests, the glorious leaking of political cover-ups, the deleterious effects of drugs and junk food (all glitz and little substance), the breakdown of families and a society that is terminal, and simply cannot go on living the way it is.

We are at a crucial juncture, Our 'God' has not served us and is not serving us. It is time to make some very important changes.

I hope this book will assist the reader get a deeper sense of what has gone wrong and will catalyze feelings and thoughts on what we can do to heal it.

Leo Rutherford, England, 2011.

Leo Rutherford, MA, is a truthseeker, writer and workshop facilitator, living in the UK. His life has taken many twists and turns and has shown him graphically that most everything he was taught to believe during his early formative years was crap! He constantly attempts to pull the wraps off that which is hidden and delights in pulling the rug from under those who seek to conceal, control, limit and dominate.

Chapter 1
Genesis: Beliefs and Cultural Mythologies

When you were a child were you taught all about Santa Claus/ Father Christmas, this lovely rotund old chap with a white beard who brought you presents at Christmas? And did you one day find out it was a lie, that he didn't actually exist – it was really your Mum and Dad?

Were you then taught about another white bearded even grander old chap called God and told that He really REALLY existed and that you MUST believe in Him all the rest of your life or you won't be a good person and you won't go to heaven when you die? And were you told He wrote a great big book called 'The Holy Bible' which is all his own words and all true, every single word? And that He sent 'His Only Son' to save you, and everyone else too, from all your sins? And if you don't believe all that and repeat parrot fashion what they tell you, then you'll be a bad person and not acceptable to all the nice Christian Believers and you'll have a terrible afterlife or maybe even none at all when you die?

And did you cotton on that this is a bunch of mind-control too? Or does it still try to pull at you to be a believer? Do you feel guilty if you don't at least try to believe what they tell you?

Have you questioned the accepted description of 'God'? Have you read the Bible and wondered just who wrote it and how much of it is true? Were you told there are tenets you must believe regardless of whether they make any sense to you? And were you told if you don't believe you will go to hell?

Have you felt a knowing that this is wrong? That somehow you are being conned into submission?

Have you felt that there is a much deeper purpose to human life than the daily round of working, eating, sleeping, paying bills etc? Have you felt a longing for connection to that greater something and yet not quite known just what you were longing for?

Have you felt dissatisfaction with the way your life is yet not been sure what to do to change it for the better? Wondered how we got into this mess of unsustainable over-consumption of earth's resources while many are still poor and struggle for survival?

This book is here to help you look again at cultural consensus beliefs and dissect them to see what they are, where they came from, whether they stand up to intelligent examination and whether or not they are serving you.

Cultural mythologies:

A culture interprets reality through the stories the collective tells to itself and of itself. In other words, by its mythologies and by the beliefs spawned by those myths. The stories we tell ourselves – of how things are, why it is, how it was all created and who/what is ultimately responsible for creation, are the building blocks of what we learn to see as 'reality', our consensual agreement about Life, the Universe and Everything. In the words of physicist Gary Zukav: –

"Reality is what we take to be true.

What we take to be true is what we believe.

What we believe is based upon our perceptions.

2

What we perceive depends upon what we look for.

What we look for depends upon what we think.

What we think depends upon what we perceive.

What we perceive determines what we believe.

What we believe determines what we take to be true.

What we take to be true is our reality!"

We humans have a serious tendency to accept others' beliefs about how the world is, how we should be, how and what we should 'see' and what is true and untrue. But there is a LIE in belief and it stares us in the face. BELIEF spells –

BE (in the) **LIE** (and you get) **F**(ried)

That's the polite version! When we accept other people's beliefs without checking through our own experience, we become diminished, we lose integrity, the sense of our own rights, personal sovereignty and inner power. In return we get to be accepted as a 'normal' person, one of the hive. This is the peer pressure of the mass and it is an enormous pressure. In the words of an expert:

"If you tell a lie big enough and keep repeating it, people will eventually come to believe it." Joseph Goebbels.

And the words of the two most violent 20th century dictators:

"Through clever and constant application of propaganda, people can be made to see paradise as hell, or to consider the most wretched sort of life as a paradise." Adolf Hitler.

"Print is the sharpest and the strongest weapon of our party. The writer is the engineer of the human mind." Josef Stalin.

– and a president:

"See, in my line of work you got to keep repeating things over and over and over again for the truth to sink in, to kind of catapult the propaganda." – George W. Bush, Greece, N.Y., May 24, 2005

"If this were a dictatorship, it'd be a heck of a lot easier, just so long as I'm the dictator." –Washington, D.C., Dec. 19, 2000

And a more complex exposition of the same from George Orwell: (Author of *1984* and *Animal Farm*)

"The power of holding two contradictory beliefs in one's mind simultaneously, and accepting both of them....To tell deliberate lies while genuinely believing in them, to forget any fact that has become inconvenient, and then, when it becomes necessary again, to draw it back from oblivion for just so long as it is needed, to deny the existence of objective reality and all the while to take account of the reality which one denies — all this is indispensably necessary. Even in using the word doublethink it is necessary to exercise doublethink. For by using the word one admits that one is tampering with reality; by a fresh act of doublethink one erases this knowledge; and so on indefinitely, with the lie always one leap ahead of the truth."

An ability mastered by politicians the world over!

In the thousands of years of human evolution, there have been many belief systems, frameworks, consensual 'realities,' ways of seeing this amazing world in which we live. Even today, we can travel to other cultures whose way of seeing reality is significantly different from our own.

If we stay long enough and imbibe their way of seeing and being, we can have the dubious pleasure of returning to our own culture and getting culture shock and an awakening that the beliefs, givens and assumptions of our own home land are nothing more than just that – unconscious (and semi-conscious) agreements about how to look at things and what is accepted as true and not true.

Faith and belief are not the same:

I remember watching a fascinating TV program a few years ago called 'Around the World in Eighty Faiths' in which Peter Owen Jones, a C of E Vicar, travelled the world experiencing many different ways of relating to the Source/God/Spirit. What struck me forcibly was that all the faiths were, at heart, fundamentally the same. They all recognized and sought connection with something greater than ourselves - a Source, a Force, a Creator, a Consciousness, a Zero Point, God, Divine Being – expressed in many different ways. There was no conceivable reason for any faith to make war on another faith.

However, when it came to the beliefs, the story was very different. The rules and laws for societal conduct differed enormously, the specific beliefs in what was right and what was wrong, on what their 'God' demanded and what 'S/He' might bless or curse were enormously varied. The should(n't)s, must(n't)s and ought(n'ts) were as different as the lifestyles, habitations and diets. Here was plenty of reason to feel different to and combative with other nationalities, countries, groups or tribes.

I want to make it clear that throughout this book I shall be talking of faith and belief as two different things.

Spirituality and religion are not the same either.

The prime difference between spirituality and religion is that spirituality is about finding and developing your own connection to The Source, about finding the mystic within yourself; while religion means joining a church or group and being told how to do it, what to do, what precepts and laws you must obey and what tenets you must believe. Usually you find they put priests between you and The Source.

'God' and 'Lord' are not the same either:

GOD is a shortening of the word GOOD and originally meant the beneficent power of The Universe. Lord relates to law. A lord is a lawgiver, someone who tells you what you can and cannot do, a boss-chap. 'God' (in its original meaning) relates to faith but 'lord' to belief.

Unsustainability and disconnection:

Our present Western 'civilized', 'developed', 'advanced' culture has numerous extraordinary facets. We are affecting the climate by creating unprecedented pollution of natural systems to a point where we may well take things beyond any recoverable balance; we are poisoning our own food so now 'organically grown' food – food grown without poisons or at least with less of them – is a significant item for many of us. We have produced weapons of such mass destruction which, if used, will produce untold and quite possibly irreparable devastation to our planetary home. The vast amount we collectively spend on these weapons – ostensibly to protect ourselves from each other – could be re-directed to wipe out starvation, poverty, a lot of disease and to provide plenty for all.

The degree to which very many people feel separate and alienated is reflected in the crime rate; in the misuse of alcohol & drugs. (Alcohol is a mind altering drug, it just happens to be the number one socially accepted drug of our culture); in the suicide rate (a recent statistic shows that suicide is the third highest cause of death in children aged five to seventeen in USA); in the lack of care for the environment and the breakdown of families.

If we continue on the road of everlasting economic growth, how long will it be before there are so many cars that the cities and the roads just come to a stop and the air is too foul to breathe? How long before the skies are so full of planes that there is a pollution crisis in the upper atmosphere? How long before we run out of oil? How long before we have a food crisis or a water crisis due to pollution and climate change?

One thing is sure. We live in a culture that is terminal in its present form. At some inner level most of us know this. Our youth especially see and feel little future with things the way they are. Our mythologies are not serving us. Dogmatic religious beliefs in a punitive, judgmental, warlike 'God' have seriously misled us and it is time to look closely at them.

Our leaders have no answers and simply go on re-creating the same messes. The Native American culture had an inbuilt teaching that one's present actions should take account of seven future generations. Our culture barely manages to look beyond the next election.

The Takers and the Givers:

Taker cultures – like us – take more than we give, seek continuous expansion, continuous 'economic growth', more and more of everything, seek profit in all our doings – and leave a planet sucked dry.

Giver cultures take what they need, respect the earth and her cycles, replant for the future, limit population according to what is sustainable and live with an eye always on the future of the children. It has been calculated that if everyone on the planet lived like an American, we would need something like four and half more planets to provide for us!

Somehow we need to make radical changes towards be-coming a Giver culture.

'God':

We need to start with the God(s) we worship because what we worship, revere, hold in esteem, pay homage to, seek to emulate and obey, deeply affects how we live and behave; how we 'see' our world; how we form our consensual idea of reality; how we feel about ourselves and what we agree on as the right ways to be and to live. In this book we will look at the two main strands of spiritual/religious faith and belief: the Biblical Abrahamic male-monotheist God and the 'great world religions' that have followed from 'Him', and the animist pluralist God(s) of our more ancient ancestors (and many of the remaining indigenous cultures of today) and what has followed from them. We will discuss the type of cultures, consensus belief systems and ways of living that result from the adoption of these 'God(s)'.

Animism:

The animist sees soul/spirit in everything. From the Oxford dictionary: *Animism – Doctrine of the anima mundi; attribution of living soul to inanimate objects and natural phenomena; spiritualism as opposed to materialism.*

Other definitions: A 'Heathen' – *one who sees God in the heath* – ie in nature; 'Pagan' means a *country person* – ie one who lives in, amongst and with nature; 'witch' means wise *woman* and most often a healer, herbalist, naturopath and/or soul doctor. Nothing whatsoever like the meaning Christianity attributed to it.

Animism leads people to revere the earth as a living being and therefore to care for her. It considers the plants, animals and even insects as beings with soul and that all beings have their place and are necessary in Creation or they would not have been created. This way of thinking leads to healthy ecology and balance. It would pull us away from ideas of everlasting economic growth because it would keep us in mind of the consequences of that – that we would be abusing the earth to get more out of her than she can give sustainably.

> All the earth is sacred
> Every step we take
> All the air is sacred,
> Every breath we take

Monotheism:

The monotheist God is quite different. 'He' is separate from 'His' creation which 'He' sits outside of in the place, most often, of judgment. He has 'chosen' people and many enemies, fights wars, commits genocide, demands obedience, punishes with violence – yet loves you so much and demands that you love him back – and has hell waiting for you if you don't or if you fail his commands.

In the words of comedian George Carlin:-

"Religion has actually convinced people there's an invisible man living in the sky who watches everything you do every minute of every day, and the invisible man has ten things he doesn't want you to do and if you do any of them he has a place of fire, smoke, burning, torture and anguish to send you to live where you'll suffer, burn, choke, scream and cry for ever and ever till the end of time…. BUT HE LOVES YOU….!"

I call him the 'God-Chap' because 'He' is entirely male and remarkably like a dominant/domineering patriarchal man. I suggest that our current gigantic human problems largely stem from the acceptance by many nations and too many people of this warlike, murderous, abusive, psychopathic, misogynistic

9

character as 'God'. (If you didn't like that statement, read 'His Own Words' in Chapter 4 and see what you think then.) We become like what we worship. To become a peaceful, compassionate and loving culture we first need to adopt a peaceful, compassionate and loving God.

Superstition:

I was brought up to believe that all the ancient pre-Christian ways were just old ignorant superstition and completely superseded by the Bible and Jesus Christ. My life experience has led me to the absolutely opposite conclusion. After more than thirty years of experience and study of ancient animist/shamanist ways I have found them to be based a deep understanding of nature, the cosmos and evolution. Of 'what is', not of beliefs. Here is some of what I have now come to consider superstition:

1. Jesus Christ died for your sins and only through believing in him will you be saved and have eternal life.

2. The Bible is the word of God and it is His very own holy book of instruction to the human race.

3. No one has eternal life without believing in the savior. 'Jesus is the only way to get right with God'.

4. A baby that dies before it is baptized goes to hell.

5. *The wages of sin is death'* – and this death is an eternal separation from God, in <u>hell</u>!

In this book I cast considerable doubt as to whether the Jesus as described in the Gospels ever existed in the flesh and I provide evidence for this. I quote the 'Word of God' and words of 'Jesus' (words you may not be aware of) directly from the Bible, the King James and other versions. I have come to see little connection between the 'God' described in much of the Bible and the Holy Spirit/Great Spirit Creator/Creation embraced by our more ancient ancestors.

Creation Stories:

All the ancient animist cultures I have researched, even though their creation stories differ in detail, feature a similar fundamental understanding of how things are and how the Universe works. The Creation IS the Creator in Manifestation. God, Infinite Creator, Primal Being, All-Mighty, The One, All-One, Alone, All-That-Is, became and is The Creation. They understood that there is no separation. Infinite Creator and Creation are One. All-Is-One.

That means all humans are sons and daughters of God, all animals are animals of God. Trees are trees of God, planets are Planets of God and stars are Suns of God.

Not at all like the male-monotheistic teaching which says only humans have souls and until about 450 years ago, only men, not even women! (See chapter 9) This means that every-thing else is dead, has no soul essence, and therefore can be used and abused with impunity. Hence chickens imprisoned in batteries, cattle force fed hormones till they become unnatural shapes, the earth mined and desecrated – no problem, 'god' doesn't care so why should we?

Organized religions:

There are only three organized religions in the full sense of the phrase. These are Judaism, Christianity and Islam and they all come from the Abrahamic male-monotheist root and are developments of each other. Their antecedents are the desert tribes of the Middle East and the Hiksos of Egypt.

Buddhism is not strictly a religion because it is a path rather than a belief system. Hinduism is a grey area because it can be called a religion yet is not focused on specific beliefs and a single God in the way of the three monotheistic religions who hold belief in One Male God-Chap as central and essential.

While Judaism is the religion of the Jews, Christianity and Islam are not limited by race considerations. They both teach that they have 'The Truth' and are proselytizing religions in that they feel it is their duty to convert others to their 'true faith' with the ideal that everyone will ultimately join them and believe what they say.

What will then be achieved? What else but that thing so sought by dictators, kings and fuhrers throughout the centuries – world domination through mind control and conformity!

Here is a partial list of what the male-monotheist religions achieve for you:

1. Separate you from Spirit and put priests in between.

2. Take away your earth connection and teach you the earth is irrelevant or even evil.

3. Teach you that you are sinful from birth and have to earn a place in the afterlife by doing what they tell you.

4. Take away your inner power and self-regard and teach you to doubt your self

5. Bring you into a group of fellow believers/ sinners/ followers and make you accept their beliefs as the price for inclusion.

6. If you are one of the 5% to 10% of humans born naturally homosexual, they will teach you to be at war with your own nature.

It is worth remembering that there are two major Christianities – Catholicism and Protestantism (and many other subsections) and there are two Islams – the Sunni and Shia. In both cases they have fought and killed each other, the Sunni and Shia for more than 1350 years.

I was taught to believe that religion is about peace and love. Were you?

The Mystics were very different:

All three religions have two separate divisions, the external religions who tell their members what to believe, what to do and how to live, and the mystics who have received ecstatic revelations and who teach inner knowledge. For the Jews this is the Kabbalah, for the Islamists it is the Sufis and for the Christians it is the Christian mystics such as Meister Eckhart and Hildegard of Bingen. Here is Meister Eckhart (1260-1329): –

"God is infinite in his simplicity and simple in his infinity. Therefore he is everywhere and is everywhere complete. He is everywhere on account of his infinity, and is everywhere complete on account of his simplicity. Only God flows into all things, their very essences. Nothing else flows into something else. God is in the innermost part of each and every thing, only in its innermost part." [Sermon LW XXIX] From Meister Eckhart, *Selected Writings*, translated by Oliver Davies, Penguin Books, 1994.

Eckhart... stressed the unity of God and the capacity of the individual soul to become one with God during life. He said that the human soul was superior to the angels. And he spoke of passing beyond God to a `simple ground', a `still desert', without any distinctions, out of which all things were created – a conception strikingly similar to the Tao of Lao Tzu. *http://www. pantheism.net/paul/eckhart.htm*)

Here are words from Hildegard of Bingen (1098-1179):

"God's Word is in all creation, visible and invisible.
The Word is living, being,
spirit, all verdant greening,
all creativity.
This Word flashes out in
every creature.
This is how the spirit is in
the flesh—the Word is indivisible from God."

"When a woman is making love with a man, a sense of heat
in her brain, which brings with it sensual delight, communicates the
taste of that delight during the act and summons forth the emission
of the man's seed. And when the seed has fallen into its place, that
vehement heat descending from her brain draws the seed to itself
and holds it, and soon the woman's sexual organs contract, and all
the parts that are ready to open up during the time of menstrua-
tion now close, in the same way as a strong man can hold some-
thing enclosed in his fist."

These inspirational writings of the mystics show how far
the external church has come from its essence and how close
the mystics are to the animists of old. I suggest that today we
are at a place in evolution where we are called to find the mystic within; that it is our task to make our own connection to
the Source and to bypass churches and religious organizations
(corporations) which want to take our power and our money;
that demand our fealty and give us all sorts of rules and laws
which they demand we believe, accept and obey.

Isn't it quite something to consider that every organised
religion with all its rules and laws started out as a mystic's
revelation?

Genesis:

"In the beginning was the word and the word was with God and the word was God." (John 1:1)

Translation: In the beginning was consciousness, and consciousness was with God and consciousness was (and is) God.

Or we can substitute *awareness* or perhaps *vibration, sound* or *beingness* or even existence.

"In the beginning was Existence and Existence was with God, and Existence was (and is) God."

In the beginning was existence /awareness /consciousness / vibration /sound /– and that was (and is) 'God'. Ooommmmm.........

That makes sense with the much older understandings: that 'God' means All-That-Is and Ever-Was and Ever-Will-Be. There is nothing else, never has been and never can be.

Now in the first Genesis story, God creates the world in seven days in a delightful apocryphal story that some religionists want to take as word-for-word literal truth. As if there were 'days' before Creation! The human ability for absurdity amazes. Here is some more –

In 1650, a certain James Ussher, Archbishop of Armagh in Ireland, published the *Annales Veteris Testamenti*, which became a Church-approved 'Universal History.' It stated that God completed his creation on 21st of September, 4004 BC (Some records say October) in the evening. To achieve such accuracy as to be able to pinpoint it to very time of day so long ago is truly astonishing! Well, one thing is for certain. God cannot have been British or he would have finished by 4 o'clock in time for a nice cup of Darjeeling tea, a cucumber sandwich and a piece of cinnamon cake....

However, whatever the truth might or might not be was deemed quite irrelevant in 1654 (that's only 357 years ago!) because the Vatican Council decreed that anyone found not believing that the world was created in 4004 BC was a heretic and would be treated as such. Which could mean being burned at the stake or murdered in some equally appalling church-sanctioned way. Or, at the very least, made stateless and having all your worldly good confiscated for the benefit of the priests. (Nice easy way to get rich!) Comically, this edict was not repealed until 1952!

This is our history, folks. A mere 350 odd years ago, people could be murdered or rendered stateless by their church for not believing a load of obviously (to any faintly intelligent person) absurd crap!

Professor Dan Smail is a medievalist with Harvard University's History Department who says that our chronology of the human race is embarrassingly out of date. He says we need to move the starting date back about 100,000 years! (*American Historical Review*, 2006.)

Quoted in *Nexus Magazine* April 2006: *"According to the history books, civilization as we know it had its first stirrings in the Fertile Crescent around 4000 – 6000 BC. But as Smail points out in an article in the latest issue of the American Historical Review, when you consider recent (and no so recent) discoveries in archeology, anthropology and biology – the finding that all humankind can be traced to Africa, for example, or that humans were on the march out of that continent by roughly 100,000 BC not to mention good guesses for when language, hunting and farming arose – the fixation on a starting date of 4000 – 6000 BC begins to seem awfully arbitrary."* (He is so polite – he means it's a load of idiotic codswallop!)

There is a kind of mad logic about Bishop Ussher's date, however. It must have been around that time that man – and I do mean MAN – invented 'god' in his (worst) image, drove out the more matriarchal and less warlike cultures and started taking over the world by conquest. Since then, we have had constant war, empires building up and being destroyed, strife, competition for land and resources, killing, murder, ethnic 'cleansing' and all such evils we are familiar with. Riane Eisler wrote in detail about this in her most informative work: '*The Chalice and the Blade*'. The big issue right now is that if we don't grow up out of these appalling patriarchal domination beliefs, we may well terminate ourselves. This is the endgame and the most extreme religious nuts are calling it the 'Rapture'. They think they will be elevated to 'heaven' while the rest of us burn in hell as the planet is devastated. And they call their God a 'loving god'.

Oh the glories of hypocrisy! (Much more in Chapter 12)

Chapter 2
Creation Stories 1 and 2

In the first Bible story, God creates things in the right order and humans come last, created in God's image *male and female created he them.* (Gen 1:27)

Then comes a very much misunderstood verse, probably heavily mistranslated, but whether or not, it has been a source of ghastly human action against our planet and her kingdoms for centuries. Gen 1:28: *"Be fruitful and become many and fill the earth, and* **subdue it and have in subjection** *the fish of the sea and the flying creatures of the heavens and every living creature that is moving upon the earth."*

So the Bible-God-Chap appears to support the raping of the planet irrespective of the damage to the ecosystem. Surely there has been a serious mistranslation. To say nothing of a monstrous misuse of the Earth and her kingdoms encouraged by this statement.

Now this next bit is really strange when you think about it. In Genesis 2:7, God starts creation all over again and this time forms a man out of dust and woman out of his rib. Something has gone massively wrong here. We have two different creation stories and they don't agree at all. We have one story of logical creation which is followed by the Garden of Eden story where creation is put in a cockeyed order. This story has been a source of absurd back-to-front mythology and massive denigration of woman, of planet Earth, and of all things feminine.

Robert Graves, in his book Hebrew Myths: The book of Genesis sums up the order of the two stories:

Genesis 1	Genesis 2
Heaven	Earth
Earth	Heaven
Light	Mist
Firmament (the asteroid belt)	Man
Dry land	Trees
Grasses and trees	Rivers
Luminaries	Beasts and cattle
Sea-beasts	Birds
Birds	Woman
Cattle, creeping things, beasts	
Man and woman	

Just look where woman is placed in Genesis 2! How conveniently misogynist. And man created before the trees and rivers, beasts and cattle! What on earth was he supposed to have lived on? The big problem is that it is the second story that feeds into the rest of the Bible, not the first. It seems to me that the God of Genesis 1 is not the same as the God of Genesis 2 and the rest of the Bible. Somehow there has been a switch – and we've got lumbered with the wrong 'God'. So let us now look in some detail at this strange second myth:

The Myth of Adam and Eve:

Here are passages from the KJV of Genesis: (Please bypass if you already know them)

2:8-9: And the LORD God planted a garden eastward in Eden; and there he put the man whom he had formed. And out of the ground made the LORD God to grow every tree that is pleasant to the sight, and good for food; the tree of life also in the midst of the garden, and the tree of knowledge of good and evil.

2:15-25: And the LORD God took the man, and put him into the garden of Eden to dress it and to keep it. And the LORD God commanded the man, saying, Of every tree of the garden thou mayest freely eat:

But of the tree of the knowledge of good and evil, thou shalt not eat of it: for in the day that thou eatest thereof thou shalt surely die.

And the LORD God said, It is not good that the man should be alone; I will make him an help meet for him.

And out of the ground the LORD God formed every beast of the field, and every fowl of the air; and brought them unto Adam to see what he would call them: and whatsoever Adam called every living creature, that was the name thereof.

And Adam gave names to all cattle, and to the fowl of the air, and to every beast of the field; but for Adam there was not found an help meet for him.

And the LORD God caused a deep sleep to fall upon Adam, and he slept: and he took one of his ribs, and closed up the flesh instead thereof;

And the rib, which the LORD God had taken from man, made he a woman, and brought her unto the man.

And Adam said, This is now bone of my bones, and flesh of my flesh: she shall be called Woman, because she was taken out of Man.

Therefore shall a man leave his father and his mother, and shall cleave unto his wife: and they shall be one flesh.

And they were both naked, the man and his wife, and were not ashamed.

(Now why on earth should the concept of shame arise here? This shows the attitude of the culture of the writer)

Chapter Three continues:

Now the serpent was more subtle than any beast of the field which the LORD God had made. And he said unto the woman, Yea, hath God said, Ye shall not eat of every tree of the garden?

And the woman said unto the serpent, We may eat of the fruit of the trees of the garden:

But of the fruit of the tree which is in the midst of the garden, God hath said, Ye shall not eat of it, neither shall ye touch it, lest ye die.

And the serpent said unto the woman, Ye shall not surely die:

For God doth know that in the day ye eat thereof, then your eyes shall be opened, and ye shall be as gods, knowing good and evil.

And when the woman saw that the tree was good for food, and that it was pleasant to the eyes, and a tree to be desired to make one wise, she took of the fruit thereof, and did eat, and gave also unto her husband with her; and he did eat.

And the eyes of them both were opened, and they knew that they were naked; and they sewed fig leaves together, and made themselves aprons.

(Again – the shame inherent in the culture of that time and place shows itself)

And they heard the voice of the LORD God walking in the garden in the cool of the day: and Adam and his wife hid themselves from the presence of the LORD God amongst the trees of the garden.

And the LORD God called unto Adam, and said unto him, Where art thou?

And he said, I heard thy voice in the garden, and I was afraid, because I was naked; and I hid myself.

And he said, Who told thee that thou wast naked? Hast thou eaten of the tree, whereof I commanded thee that thou shouldest not eat?

And the man said, The woman whom thou gavest to be with me, she gave me of the tree, and I did eat.

And the LORD God said unto the woman, What is this that thou hast done? And the woman said, The serpent beguiled me, and I did eat.

And the LORD God said unto the serpent, Because thou hast done this, thou art cursed above all cattle, and above every beast of the field; upon thy belly shalt thou go, and dust shalt thou eat all the days of thy life:

And I will put enmity between thee and the woman, and between thy seed and her seed; it shall bruise thy head, and thou shalt bruise his heel.

Unto the woman he said, I will greatly multiply thy sorrow and thy conception; in sorrow thou shalt bring forth children; and thy desire shall be to thy husband, and he shall rule over thee.

And unto Adam he said, Because thou hast hearkened unto the voice of thy wife, and hast eaten of the tree, of which I commanded thee, saying, Thou shalt not eat of it: cursed is the ground for thy sake; in sorrow shalt thou eat of it all the days of thy life;

Thorns also and thistles shall it bring forth to thee; and thou shalt eat the herb of the field;

In the sweat of thy face shalt thou eat bread, till thou return unto the ground; for out of it wast thou taken: for dust thou art, and unto dust shalt thou return.

(And this is a Loving God??)

And Adam called his wife's name Eve; because she was the mother of all living.

Unto Adam also and to his wife did the LORD God make coats of skins, and clothed them.

And the LORD God said, Behold, the man is become as one of us, to know good and evil: and now, lest he put forth his hand, and take also of the tree of life, and eat, and live for ever.

Therefore the LORD God sent him forth from the garden of Eden, to till the ground from whence he was taken.

So he drove out the man; and he placed at the east of the garden of Eden Cherubims, and a flaming sword which turned every way, to keep the way of the tree of life.

There are many strange things about this myth. The 'Voice of God' is just like that of a man, not God at all! The myth says Jehovah-God (whoever he is) made the garden, put the best bit in the center, and then said to Adam, "You can't touch that."

Now come on – every parent knows what happens if you give a child a room full of toys, put the best in the middle and say you can't play with that one. I mean whoever wrote this have must been joking … or abysmally stupid!

Then Jehovah takes a rib from Adam and creates Eve. Well, that's the only time in any history anywhere that man has given birth to woman. On every other occasion, woman gives birth. Nowhere on earth, in any recorded history, has a male given birth! Never, nowhere, no when, no how! Then the story gets weirder.

Genesis 2:25: '*They were both naked and ashamed.*' Shame again. Oh, but the Bible is the word of God isn't it, so that must mean God was ashamed! Ashamed of his own creation? Ever more peculiar!

Then along comes the cunning old Serpent, and knowingly asks Eve if God has forbidden her from eating any of the fruits of the trees. Obviously, he knows the score full well. He then suggests to Eve that God is lying and she will not die if she eats of the tree of knowledge. So she goes right ahead and eats and 'her eyes are opened.' And she doesn't die which shows 'God' <u>was</u> lying!

Now there is something rather important that would not have happened if Eve had obeyed God and *not* eaten of the Tree of the Knowledge of Good and Evil.

Think now, Ask yourself what, or who would not exist?

Something quite crucial and important would *not* exist if the Serpent hadn't successfully tempted, and Eve and Adam hadn't eaten, and their 'eyes had *not* been opened.'

Now I ask you – what would not have happened? Think about it, but think BIG. In fact think MEGA. Something mega important would not have happened and something mega important would not exist.

Ask yourself – what would not exist?

Go to the next page when you've got it ...

YOU!

ME!

AND THE WHOLE HUMAN RACE!

This story tells mythologically of the birth of human consciousness. Without the knowledge of good and evil, we are not human. Without this blessing – and challenge – of self-awareness, of knowing 'I,' we would not have the power of conscious choice and the experience of knowingly reaping the results of our actions. We would not look in a mirror and recognize our Self.

So the religionists, by screwing up this story, are actually promoting anti-evolution, actually castigating the last great evolutionary development or 'enlightenment' that took place on planet Earth, actually saying we shouldn't have become aware! Shouldn't have become human! Should have stayed animals because that's what their 'God' wanted! And we are forever guilty because we dared to take that evolutionary step. Astonishing!

And they tell us to blame the Serpent and Eve. From the point of view of evolution, the Serpent and Eve are the *good guys* and 'God' is the *bad guy*. Think about it ....

Animals don't know good and evil. Plants don't know good and evil. Planets, rocks and soil don't know good and evil. Only humans know good and evil. Only humans have the power of conscious choice to do good or harm. Human choice is a greatly challenging thing. We all know how much appalling harm has been done by 'good people' for the sake of 'God' with all the seeming best intentions in the world. How about the Crusades? Religious wars? Burning alive of people they called heretics and witches – thousands of them over centuries. Or the total wipeout (genocide) in the twelfth century of the Cathars of Southern France by the Catholic Church?

Or the genocide of the Hittites and others who lived in the 'Promised Land' which 'God' 'gave' to the Israelites. Or the appalling centuries of the Unholy Inquisition. (See Chapter 9 for more on these iniquities.)

Only humans bear the 'cross' of conscious choice and the responsibility that goes with it. It is the mark of being human. Look how our cultural myths have been messed with.

Consider this phrase: 'The knowledge of good and evil.'

Many religionists understood this as meaning the knowledge of Good-God-Spirit and the knowledge of Evil-Primal-Mother-Earth.

We live in a strange world with some very strange ideas accepted as 'normal.' Look again at the everyday words GOOD and EVIL.

'Good' spells God but with an 'o' missing!

'Evil' relates to Eve - primal woman.

Eve is primal woman in the myth we have just told. And her name, through the misinterpretation of the Adam and Eve story, has been related to all the badness in the world. Isn't that strange? How can woman be bad? Woman gives birth, all of us humans are born of woman. And yet the very name of the primal woman has been taken to represent all things bad.

The ultimate Primal woman is Mother Earth, our planet. The word 'evil' then implies the doings of the Earth, our Mother. This means that all 'good' supposedly comes from 'God,' which implies the non-manifest realm, and all 'bad' comes from the Earth, the manifest realm in which we live.

Now if we look back on religious thought of the last 2000 years and more, much of it – as I will graphically show in later chapters – has been about rejection of the earth, the body, and all things physical in favor of the 'heavens' and all (non) things

27

spiritual. With a mindset that does not value the physical realm, is it any wonder then that we have trashed our earth and our atmosphere; created nutritionally empty convenience foods that contain pesticide residues and poisonous preservatives; created a mass of convenience vehicles that spew poisons out of their exhausts; worst of all created weapons of mass destruction which, if fully utilized will terminate most life on the earth. This is the essence of the culture we have inherited, have still got, and have the enormous task of changing before it gets taken to its ultimate deathly conclusion.

It wasn't always like this: According to Gayle S. Myers (1991),

"There is enormous archeological evidence which indicates that in older times God was thought of as a woman, the Great Mother. Revered for centuries, she was the one who gave birth to all life in the Universe. She was the fertile vessel of sexuality and creativity regarded as sacred and central to life.

"New archeological finds suggest that these early mother worshipping societies had everything necessary for civilization from art to sanitation, farming, they manufactured and governed in cultures that were as advanced as early Greeks. The only thing missing from their societies was the weapons of warfare. Their cities, equipped with every thing from temples to sewage pipes had no defensive walls and their burial sites contained no aggressive weapons. It seems they were both advanced and peaceful.

"With God as the Great Mother, the values espoused were what you would expect from a good mother. Nurturing, compassion, co-operation and an acute reverence for life was the foundation for these ancient feminine centered religions.

('Mother I feel you under my feet,

Mother I hear your heart beat')

"Ishtar, Innana, Isis, Kali, the Great Mother was a deity of vast regions including central Europe, Mediterranean and India. Stable and thriving for 2500 years.

"Games and activities depicted in art indicate a valuing of both genders.

"Change came between 2000 and 1000 BC when destabilized by natural disasters – earthquakes and volcanic eruptions, warlike northern nomads – Aryans – migrated south and with their weaponry easily decimated the peaceful agrarian Goddess cultures. Their religious motifs centered around the blade which they obviously regarded as sacred.

"These conquerors brought their male-dominated religions. The once ruling Great Mother was reduced to wife or consort of the ruling male deity. The values of the invaders, in contrast to nurturing, co-operation and the ability to create life, centered around power, warfare and the ability to take life."

They banished the feminine from her rightful place in the Trinity, leaving only the masculine, and sadly their beliefs are still widely held in this so-called 'advanced' time. No wonder so many in our 'developed' world are suffering badly from unhappiness and depression.

Here are some interesting reflections on pre-Roman and pre-Christian British history from writer/researcher Manda Scott, author of the Boudica series. (See resources) Interviewed in Sacred Hoop magazine Issue 70, 2010

"Boudica... comes from the era of a kind of equality, of spiritual veracity, to which we have not yet returned. We're still suffering from the entire Roman project that began with the destruction of our culture and the creation of the patriarchal domestic, urban horror that followed it. And the Christianity that was layered on top.

I discovered we were the best metal and gold crafters in the world – nobody could match us for at least the next thousand years. I learned we were an incredibly productive, artistic society, that we were producing more grain in southeast England before the Roman invasion than at any time up to the end of the First World War when petrochemicals drove agriculture yields upwards.

Thus gradually the Roman image of illiterate barbarian tribes fell away. I learned that the Druidic College on Anglesey was famed throughout the empire and that men and women went to train there for between 12 and 20 years before returning to their tribes as the mediators between the gods and their people… I learned that even 400 years later we still hadn't got used to the bizarre idea of marriage in which a woman becomes her husband's property."

A very different picture of ancient Britain prior to the devastation wrought on our ancestors by the Romans and their church.

Genesis Chapters 3 & 4:

Jehovah-God in Genesis 3: 15-16:

"And I shall put enmity between you and the woman and between your seed and her seed. He will bruise you in the head, and you will bruise him in the heel.

To the woman he said: "I shall greatly increase the pain of your pregnancy. In birth pangs you will bring forth children and your craving will be for your husband and he will dominate you."

A rare level of misogyny! And that is 'God' speaking?

In chapter 4 Abraham had two sons, Cain and Abel, and later in the story they bring their offerings to Jehovah-God. Jehovah looks with favor on Abel who herded sheep but not on Cain who tilled the ground. Very strange thing for a 'loving God' to do. Cain, in rage, then kills Abel.

Cain becomes a fugitive and goes to live east of Eden with – guess who – *other people!* He even marries one of them.

That's right – *other people!* So the Garden of Eden story is not about the only people and Jehovah-God is not the only God, just a minor bit-player, one of many.

That is really important – the Old Testament God is NOT the Almightly God at all, he is just one of several!

(Note that the word *Elohim* which was used before the word *God* is a plural term.)

It is also important to realize that only certain people have been 'thrown out of the garden'. There are lots of *other people* who still live on the earth as a garden and do not carry with them that incredible burden of shame, guilt and blame and the concept that they are inherently evil.

Imagine living without all that guilt! You were not born in sin! The death of Jesus doesn't hang on your shoulders! You don't have to believe in 'him' or else you will be damned and go to hell for eternity. What freedom!

Let us put the Serpent back in his/her rightful place and Eve, the Great Mother, back in her place of honor in the Trinity where she most essentially belongs, and return balance and harmony to our mythology so that the feminine and masculine can once again be in equal partnership ...

Now here is something else to think about: –

Long before the Bible was put together there were clay tablets from the Sumerian culture which told of a very different story of creation:

"Only during the reign of Queen Victoria did the knowledge and interest in the great Sumerian civilization begin to be revealed from the archaeological evidence, which included precisely inscribed

'cuneiform' text (wedge shaped lines) on thousands of clay tablets recovered from the remains of the ruined libraries of a cultured and ordered society, which was in full flower more than 2000 years before the old testament bible stories were compiled between 850 BC and 550 BC.

Some ancient historians did refer to the Elohim by name, but we have never been sure who was responsible for the spectacular agricultural production, monumental structures and the resulting highly organised city states, which would now appear to have existed throughout the fertile crescent and as far back as **8,000 BC** *at Jericho and Baalbek.*

It is now known that commercial accounting tokens or tablets go back to these earliest dates. Translating the cuneiform, which had changed from simple pictorial signs with an associated phonetic sound, then turned on its side to become elaborate texts supervised by professional scribes, has presented problems. Single words often have more than one meaning depending upon the context in which they are used.

Up to now some of the more solid information we have from the later Assyrian records indicate that there was a small group of wise sages called the ab-kar-llu, who passed down their wisdom to subsequent generations. The linguistic roots and phonetic sounds of the name Elohim, these sages and that of the more commonly recognised angel en-ge-li offer several logical and linked interpretations.

These words mean, respectively, the bright or shining ones (gods), the bright or shining farmers from the enclosure or garden, and the shining countenanced lords of the cultivation.

Many of the earliest biblical names end in el, the common root of bright or shining and also meaning singular god or lord, but the first part of the name probably denoted their role rather than the individual within a highly organised group displaying advanced technical and administrative skills."

(From 'The Genius of the Few' by Christian and Barbara Joy O'Brien. Also fascinating on this topic are the books of Zecharia Sitchin. See Resources)

Who were the 'Shining Ones', the Elohim? One thing is for sure – they were not God-The-Creator-Of-All-That-Is – they were an advanced race but with personalities just like us. They taught our ancestors and they have been mistaken for the real God. ~

■ An error of monumental proportions

Here is a re-translation of Genesis 1:25

From the Jerusalem Bible: "*God made every kind of wild beast, every kind of cattle and every kind of reptile. God saw that it was good.*"

Modern, critical interpretation of the earliest Hebrew Text and an alternative Genesis: "*The Elohim busied themselves with (cared for) all kinds of wildlife on the land and all kinds of domestic animals which were plentiful on the ground. The Elohim took delight in them all.*"

In the rest of this book I attempt to put this monumental error right and separate the Real Creator-God-of All-Things-Who-Is-The-Creation from the Biblical Big-Daddy-in-the-Sky God-Chap who sits in judgment, spreads guilt, revels in war and hates women, sex, and the human body!

NOTE: Some people who are familiar with this knowledge seem to think it's hardly necessary in this day and age to write a book about this – everyone knows it already. WRONG! It is reckoned that no less than 40% of Americans still believe the Bible is the literal word of God. Here in UK, I counted no less than fourteen God-Chap channels on Sky TV compared to one part-time underfunded Holistic/Alternative channel. The Roman Catholic Church claims over a billion members even after all its scandals.

Yes – it is necessary, very necessary, to spread knowledge and wisdom and show the warlike, bloodthirsty, genocidal words of the Bible and to deconstruct the false imposter male-monotheist 'god-chap' that we have been misled (conned?) to treat as if 'He' was the Creator of All-That-Is.

Chapter 3
The iniquitous concept of Original Sin

When I was growing up they told me I was born in sin and Jesus died to 'save me from my sins.' Really? Was I that bad? What was so wrong with me? Was I evil just because I was a small boy and played around and didn't always obey everyone?

That was before puberty. Once puberty struck, suddenly I had this big enormous guilty secret right there between my legs that no one talked about; that I couldn't tell anyone about; that I mustn't touch and that seemed to have an agenda all of its own! Suddenly I was out of control, wicked, guilty, the devil had got right inside of me – and I knew... I was baaaad!

How was puberty for you?

Consider your time of puberty. Was your first menstrual blood celebrated? Your first, probably spontaneous, orgasm? Were you instructed by the priest or elder in how to use your newly developing body? Told what the new and growing bits were for? How to work with this incredible energy in good, healthy, loving ways? How to give and receive pleasure beautifully?

In your dreams, I guess, but if you had been a Native American living in a tribe that had maintained its balance and harmony with the Universe and with its ancestral teachings, you would have been taught at puberty by a tribal elder – male or female appropriately – who would have instructed you in how to use and develop this energy in beauty, how to access beautiful states of consciousness with it, how to create or not create children, how to give and receive pleasure, joy and happiness with a loving partner. Consider what an incredible difference that would have made to your life.

It certainly would have to mine!

Male-monotheist literalist religions have absolutely no idea how to handle puberty! They demonize sex as something to control, limit, restrict, bottle-up and de-humanize. What is so ridiculous is that it's a demonization of the very energy through which our body forms are created! Religion demonizes the immensely powerful energy of sex and then offers to *save* us from all the resulting enormous problems they created in the first place! Well, it has kept them in business for many hundreds of years, but at what cost to the human race?

Natural sex takes us into the realms of the transcendental, of the unknown, the liminal, the chaotic. By its very nature, it takes us beyond control of the mind into a place where spirit can move us. Good sex raises our energy from the base chakra (base of the spine), to the heart and right up to the lotus (top of the head) and brings us to a place of momentary openness to Creation. Control and limit the expression of the base energy and you limit all the other energy in a person. People with low energy and low self-esteem are insecure, more obedient, more controllable and less trouble than those with high energy who feel good about themselves. By putting normal people at war with themselves, by inhibiting their natural sexual, creative vibrant self-expression, you achieve the control that Stalinists, Hitlerists and fascists of all shapes and sizes have sought to do throughout history ... and with far less trouble and cost.

In my ignorance of youth, I picked up the fundamental Christian belief system, especially about sex. Today I feel ashamed that I could have been so duped. I grew up terrified of my own sexuality and power and I walked my adolescent world on eggshells like a real wimp. I have to admit to still holding a measure of anger and resentment against those who taught me such garbage, and the religious progenitors of the garbage itself. Perhaps that is (or will become) obvious in the text of this book. Well, at least I'm now putting it to good use!

Remember the adage: *Make love not war*. You can reverse that too – *Make war not love* – and that is what male-monotheist Bible teaching has been putting over all these years. Frustrate your loving, bottle up your sex because its 'bad', feel guilty when you fail, be at war with yourself – *and you will be a good soldier, my son.*

Consider the meaning of 'sin':

In Aramaic, the word 'sin' meant 'missing the mark.' It was an archery term used when missing the center of a target, missing a point, missing a kill. Put another way, it meant being off center, off the mark, making a mistake.

A person who misses the mark, who is off-center, who makes a mistake, is a normal person. Who doesn't make mistakes? Putting that in the old language, one can ask: 'Who isn't a sinner?'

Answer: No one! We all make mistakes, we all get off-center, we all miss the mark. Hopefully we hit as often as we miss. And the more we live, experience, learn from life, learn to live well, to live in a state of lovingness, the more we hit the mark and the fewer mistakes we make. That, in the old language, is to sin less. An airplane flying from, let's say, London to New York, spends over 90% of its time off-course, but by regular course adjustments, gets there just fine. The airplane 'sins' for 90% of its journey, yet succeeds perfectly in doing its job!

So it is with ourselves as we continuously learn from life and evolve our course.

But now if one man dies for the sins of all others, what does that mean? That all your previous mistakes (sins) are eradicated? That you no longer need to learn from life? That you now have no need for further knowledge, further experience, further learning, further exploring? That 'He' did it all for you? And all you have to do is believe?

This makes no sense whatsoever, it is like saying you should remain a dependent child all your life. A life without learning, growth, development, exploration, change, flowering, and all that implies, is no life. It has no point.

This nonsense makes all personal development and growth unnecessary and irrelevant. If we are not here to grow and develop, then what are we born for? Forget schools and universities, books and study, knowledge and wisdom, and just replace it all with a set of rigid dogmatic beliefs! AAH! But they already did that and created the Dark Ages by burning books and libraries and enforcing ignorance on pain of death. Message: Read *only* the Bible, stay ignorant and be controlled by us.

Mind you, there is one hell of a problem for 'true believers.' What about all the millions of humans who existed before Jesus? He wasn't around then for them to believe in and he certainly wasn't around to 'save' them. The Catholic Church realized they had a big problem with this and to solve it they said that all good Christians, (that means good rigid dogmatic Catholics only - of course) who lived before Jesus, went into a sort of limbo holding pattern after death until the end of time. It seems someone twigged that Moses, Abraham and all sorts of worthies had been in Catholic 'limbo' for a massively long time, and just recently the Pope thought it was time they were let out … only it still leaves the churches teaching on this matter rather in – er – limbo….

It seems also that the Catholic Church holds that however you sin while in life, so long as you confess and repent on your deathbed and commit yourself to Jesus – as a committed Catholic, of course – you can still get a place reserved for you in 'heaven' when you shuffle off the mortal coil. What a load of old manipulation and bribery! Do as thou wilt until the last, and just be sure to change your tune on your deathbed. Easypeazy!

Popes of old used to increase their coffers by selling 'indulgences,' so there was no need to get too serious about the daily problems of sin. (Sounds rather like the UK scandal of selling dukedoms for political donations.) I recently read that Ratzinger-Pope is re-activating this. (Does he need the money?)

What astonishes me is that no one seems to see what a total and utter ridiculing of the Creator this is. Doing deals with God?? It makes 'God' into the most appalling, small-minded, bigoted, unseeing human-like moron. Male, of course! And this is supposed to be the Creator of the Whole Universe? What an insult of megalithic proportions!

Born in sin?

Isn't it a seriously peculiar idea that all humans should be born in sin? Have you ever looked properly at a new born child in its natural beauty? Doesn't it move something in your heart when you see a very little child? Can you be serious and say this child is born in sin? What a ridiculous, damaging, absurd, abominable tenet this is. How *huge* has been the emotional damage done to people who believed such an appallingly soul-destroying/self-negating concept? How much hurt and pain has this abomination caused in the last millennias?

From Psalm 51:5:

"Behold I was shapen in wickedness: in this sin hath my mother conceived me."

In the 1st century, Tertullian (Quintus Florens Tertullianus, 155-220, influential Christian writer and father of the church) wrote:

"Each of you women is an Eve...You are the gate of Hell, you are the temptress of the forbidden tree; you are the first deserter of the divine law."

He also declared:

"Chastity is a means whereby a man will traffic in a mighty substance of sanctity." And that the sexual act rendered even marriage obscene.

He must have had a lot of sexual frustration in his life!

St Jerome: *"Regard everything as poison which bears within it the seed of sensual pleasure."*

Later on in the 16th century, Martin Luther decreed:

"If a woman grows weary and at last dies from childbearing, it matters not. Let her die from bearing, she is there to do it."

Misogyny of a rare sort. Perhaps he hated his mother! Here is another piece of horrible anti-woman preaching from a New England minister, circa 1800's (reported by Barbara G Walker in *The Woman's Encyclopedia of Myths and Secrets*, Harper and Row, 1983):

"Chloroform is a decoy of Satan, apparently offering itself to bless women; but in the end it will harden society and rob God of the deep earnest cries which arise in time of trouble, for help."

John Calvin (1509-64) clearly hated children and women. Reading his stuff makes you wonder just what sort of parenting he must have had, to say nothing of a love-life. Here is an example of his teaching:

"Even infants bring their condemnation with them from the mother's womb ... their whole nature is ... a seed of sin ... and odious and abominable to God."

A baby odious and abominable to God? Just what on earth does he think of his god? From the 4th century, Catholic theologian St. Augustine said:

"Do not believe, or say, or teach, that the unbaptized infant can be forgiven original sin—not if you wish to be a Catholic."

This absurd doctrine means that babies must be baptized in order for them to have a chance at 'salvation', or else they cannot go to 'heaven' when they die. And this means if a fetus is aborted, or miscarried, it will never, ever, have a chance to be 'saved'! Hence the anti-abortion lobby. And all because of maniacal, misguided, sexually frustrated preachers. Clearly then, anti-abortionists must fanatically defend fetuses at all costs, but they don't have to be the slightest bit concerned with the already-born because it doesn't matter if people are poor or suffering or how hellish the conditions of their lives are. The only thing that matters is that they get born so they will have a chance at 'eternal salvation'!

"Even though anesthesia began to be used in 1846, it was not routinely administered to women in childbirth for almost 40 years, because many doctors followed the biblical teaching that women must suffer in childbirth."'

— Gaylor, 1981 and 1993;)

Disgusting! This is predicated on Genesis 3:16 where the 'God-Chap' says:

"To the woman he said: "I shall greatly increase the pain of your pregnancy; in birth pangs you will bring forth children, and your craving will be for your husband, and he will dominate you."

Can you really and honestly believe this is 'god' speaking? If you do believe that, what on earth do you think of your 'God'? What, I wonder, do you think 'He' thinks of you?

Orthodox Christians not only saw woman as lesser and filthy but also the act of birth itself, so that after giving birth a woman had to have a 40-day (for a boy child) or an 80-day (for a girl child) purifying or 'churching' in order to be re-admitted to the church and 'proper Christian society'. It seems that some thought even the Virgin Mary needed to be purified after giving birth to Jesus!

Incredible – but as I say – this is our history. Compare it with this from Thom Hartmann, *The Last Hours of Ancient Sunlight* (p303, Harmony Books, 1999.) Compare.... and weep:

"Hundreds of thousands of years of human history – and the modern day 'primitive' people we can still find alive on the earth – tell us that the 'conventional wisdom' that 'man's innate nature is evil and dominating' is a lie, a sickness unique to our culture, and a relatively recent sickness in the long history of the human race. ***Instead, we are born to an innate knowledge and awe of the divine in all creation, and our first and most basic instincts are compassion and love."*** (My emphasis)

Sexual mores:

Let us look now at the sexual mores put out by the church. If we take the Catholic version as the original, it basically says: "No birth control, no abortion, no masturbation, no sex outside marriage. And it (subtly?) suggests not too much within marriage unless you are intending pregnancy."

Not much left to enjoy! Sorry, you shouldn't enjoy it either, just do it as a duty when you have to!

St Augustine's recommendations for marriage were:

"*Husbands love your wives but love them chastely. Insist on the work of the flesh only in such measure as is necessary for the procreation of children. Since you cannot beget children in any other way,* **you must descend to it against your will,** *for it is the punishment of Adam.*" (Yes, that's **my emphasis!**)

Isn't that lovely? '**Descend to it against your will.**' 'Darling, come and descend with me against your will, (mine too – of course). Let us suffer together that God may quickly grant us a child without too much of this unchristly copulation curfuffle!

And I promise to get it over with as quickly as possible....'

I mean – really! Back in the Victorian era in some parts of society, it was customary to put a sheet with a small hole in it between you when you 'descended to it.' Also a Jewish habit in some parts, I understand.

Relief by masturbation? Oh no, that's a sin, we want none of that sort of thing! Why? It's all in Genesis 38:8-10.

After God killed Er, Judah tells Onan to "*Go in unto thy brother's wife. (But) Onan knew that the seed should not be his; and ... when he went in unto his brother's wife ... he spilled it on the ground....And the thing which he did displeased the Lord; wherefore he slew him also.*"

In just this little story 'God' kills Er and then Onan – and from here on, '*spilling your seed*' is counted as a major sin for men. This story is seldom (never?) read in Sunday School, but it is the basis of the Christian doctrine of no masturbation.

What on earth is a normal young mortal supposed to do with their natural sexual energy? Work against it? 'Confess' it every week as if it were 'bad'? It seems to me to be a perfect recipe for misery, unhappiness and serious inner conflict, leading to alcoholism, violence, war, pornography, rape, strife and evils of all sorts. Just about what we've got, in fact. Here's a heretical thought: How about taxing the (exceedingly wealthy) church for the costs to society of all the problems it has created?

History tells that Augustine had problems with his own sexuality. Apparently he was promiscuous in his youth and had an illegitimate child who he abandoned. He came to the view that sex was intrinsically evil. Oh, what guilt can do! Here he is again, dumping his problem on everyone:

"Who can control this when its appetite is aroused? No one!"

Well he couldn't, obviously. The fact that others can while he couldn't must have been outside his awareness, and he simply projected his own incompetence onto everybody. He goes on:

"In the very moment of the appetite, it has no mode corresponding to the will."

Of course it doesn't. It takes us beyond rationality into a wonderful, fabulous, All-One place. But Augustine, you failed to recognize that you had choice as to when to go with the appetite and when not. He goes further:

"This diabolical excitement of the genitals is evidence of Adam's original sin which is transmitted from the mother's womb and taints all human beings with sin."

So just because he couldn't control himself, he dumps sin and guilt onto all women – and all who dare to enjoy sex – and with an incredibly long-term effect too because we are still suffering from the aftermath of this griping nonsense today. And this guy is a 'saint'?

I have read that Augustine thought that God spent time before creating the world in preparing a place of punishment! Reformation preacher John Calvin says that too. Punishment first, then Creation! Astonishing.

We all know this kind of thought lives on and infects the consensus of many cultures today. Here, much later, is the Bishop of Chartres, Sir John of Salisbury quoted from *The Natural Inferiority of Women:*

"Who except one bereft of sense would approve sensual pleasure itself, which is illicit, wallows in filthiness, is something that men censure, and that God without doubt condemns?"

Today we live in a society that is severely out of balance with sexuality (as well as with femininity-masculinity), but it's important to remember that it's because of centuries of crazy religious repression, and it will not be healed by more of the same.

Here is ex-Dominican friar and Catholic priest, Matthew Fox, from *Confessions: The Making of a Post-denominational Priest* (Harper Collins, San Francisco, 1996):

"This pope and his self-appointed German Mafia headed by Cardinal Ratzinger (now Pope Benedict 16th) will have to face the judgment of history (and very likely God also) for their preoccupation with sexual morality; active encouragement of population explosion by forbidding birth control; headlong pursuit of Augustine's theology of sexuality; conscious destruction and systemic dismantling of the Liberation Theology movement with the encouragement of the CIA; the effort to eliminate theology and replace it with ideology by spreading fear among theologians; the rigid sticking to celibacy as a requisite for being a priest (as well as the requisite of having exclusively male genitals) … oh, yes, and criticizing yoga – in a prolonged effort to render fascism fashionable."

The religio-fascist repression that many people have lived under for all these centuries has been released to some degree within the last fifty to hundred years and the results are mixed to say the least. Not surprising, as there is no proper guidance and few knowledgeable guides. In the pre-monotheist religion days, this used to be the province of the elders who had wisdom and knowledge from long life experience, but we don't have those today … or incredibly few. Most of our elders are 'old people'. So our youth have little sensible guidance and must muddle through somehow as best they can.

From a letter sent by a reader of the earlier version of this book:

"I knew it was all wrong all along but couldn't realize it until I read your book spelling it all out. Even when I found myself arguing to the contrary, the next paragraph would point out the lie. Brilliant! It feels a long time since I laughed about religious twaddle, this time I laughed not only with relief but with the understanding that my path in life has turned a corner, one I needed to turn for too long.

… "And Jesus said 'suffer the little children to come unto me…'" at which point I felt I was woken up to what the teacher (a nun) was doing, little more than wanting innocent children to suffer. She even repeated it to make sure we all got the point. Original sin, my arse! I remember wondering was that why the midwife smacks the baby to make it cry when it's born as well as make its lungs start working.

…I know I need to get the crap out and let the real me emerge more. I feel I need to sweat it out, read more, talk more, listen more to good sense. I need to cry, to grieve for all that was lost, all that was taken away from me, all that should not have been."

(Rosy Gale, 2010)

For a moment, let us consider sex and swear words: –

Weapons of mass creation versus weapons of mass destruction:

Isn't it weird that many of the commonly used words to describe the sexual act in the English language are also used as swear words? Doesn't that say volumes about the Christian attitudes to sexuality?

The sexual act is the greatest single creative act we can do. We have 'Weapons of Mass Creation' with which we can do no less than reproduce ourselves. Furthermore Cosmic Design (God) has seen to it that enormous pleasure accompanies this act when it is done rightly, and enormous urges propel us regularly in its direction! Yet our words commonly used for those highly pleasurable 'weapons of mass creation' and the act they involve are desultory if not downright insulting. This is extraordinary when you think about it, and shows how far down the road to mass insanity we have come.

The words for the 'weapons of mass destruction,' on the other hand, hold no such reservation. They are easily used and no one is offended by them. So if you cross my boundaries and anger me and I say to you: 'Nuke off, you warhead', you will probably laugh and are certainly unlikely to take offence. Whereas if I translate that directly into the nearest appropriate words of mass creation and say: 'Fuck off, you prick', you may well feel offended and be stung to respond.

We consider destruction with equanimity yet equate sexual creation with embarrassment, ridicule, offence and negativity. How come? It is all part of our upside-down religious heritage, and it is way time for re-evaluation.

Consider, for a moment, the word 'fuck.' It comes from the 18th century when people were jailed for adultery and sexual misdemeanors, and their 'crime' was recorded on legal paperwork as: 'For Unlawful Carnal Knowledge'. This was abbreviated on the notice outside their cell to F.U.C.K.

Then there are words like bonk, wank, get stuffed, and so on. The male organ is derogatorily known as prick, tool, willy, john-thomas, dick etc, (Dick was a perfectly respectable man's name not that long ago) and the female organ as cunt (from cuni, Latin for birth channel, hence cuni-lingus), hole, pussy. All these words are used in a demeaning way. By contrast, the Cherokee words are Tipili (male) and Tupouli (female), the Hindi words are Vajra and Yoni and they are used in affirming, respectful and honoring ways.

Surely the bad things that happen to us are to do with war, killing, murder, ravaging, savagery, brutality, torture, destruction, decimation, so wouldn't it make more sense if our swear words reflected this? Here are some suggestions for more relevant swear words:

GET NUKED! / BOMB OFF! / EAT ANTHRAX! / GO JUMP ON A MINE! / TANK OFF / GO PLAY ON THE FREEWAY (MOTORWAY, RUNWAY) / I'LL GENETICALLY MODIFY YOU / YOU'LL BE WATERBOARDED / NUKE 'EM TILL THEY GLOW!

Feel free to add your own!

As male-monotheism took over, the feminine qualities of compassion, nurturing, caring, supporting and mutual trust went out of the window to be replaced by male competitiveness, the perceived need to 'prove' yourself, and the desire to dominate others. This was combined with lack of support leading to much loneliness, isolation and lack of self-worth. Just what I experienced at the all-male boarding school where a boy was perceived to have no value except in what he could win.

Here is an Aboriginal view described by Thom Hartmann in *The Last Hours of Ancient Sunlight* (p.242):

"When European missionaries taught Australian Aborigine hunter/gatherers how to play football (soccer) back in the early 1900s, the Aboriginal children played until both sides had equal scores: that was when the game was over, in their mind, and it boggled the British missionaries who taught them the game. The missionaries worked for over a year to convince the children that there should be winners and losers. The children lived in a matrilineal society that valued cooperation; the Englishmen came from a patriarchal society which valued domination."

With the replacement of the matriarchal cooperation and community by the patriarchal competition and domination, the human race is suffering from soul-loss on a gigantic scale. As a direct result of this our Earth-Mother is suffering from degradation, pollution, poisoning, and many forms of ecological mass destruction. If she is seen as evil and inferior, why should men (and masculinised women) bother about her?

With regard to the natural sexual instinct, imagine a Creator who puts the most powerful desire within us to engage in and enjoy sex and the most excellent rewards of loving enjoyment for doing so and then says it is a 'sin' and you mustn't do it unless you absolutely have to? Confused? Sadistic? I can't find printable words to describe my feelings. I expect some nincompoop to come waving a Bible at me and saying 'But this is the Word of God. This is what 'He' says.'

Well, have you ever read the Bible? I mean with intelligence, examining it, questioning it, not just on auto pilot? It is about the most contradictory book you can find anywhere. And violent, judgmental, warlike! Here are some extracts from the Bible that never seem to get read in church or taught in Christian circles.

It is (has been?) the cultural consensus thinking that the Bible is the actual words of God, so let us take a good look at some of 'God's' words.

Chapter 4
God in His own words

I remember in my youth being asked / told many times: "Of course, you *do believe* the Bible is the word of God, don't you?"

More a command than a question. And once they had got a yes out of me (and I didn't know any better in those days), they then proceeded to bludgeon me with selected texts that made me into a horrendous sinner and guilty for all sorts of wrongdoing, wrong thinking and devilish beliefs and quite unfit to think for myself. So naturally I should go to their church and belittle myself in front of their altar, or meekly bend over and receive their cane on my backside, or whatever demeaning actions they deemed good for my soul and captivating of my energy. By the time they had finished with me, any minuscule tendencies I might have had towards self-regard or self-confidence were well and truly swept away.

First – here is a verbatim introduction from one of those cosy Christian Bible societies:

"God reveals Himself to mankind through His Word. The Bible is a book about God and His relationship with human beings. Where do you fit in His plan? The Scriptures contain a long history of God's revelation of Himself to man—from Adam to Moses down through the apostles and the early Church. In contrast to many human assumptions, the Bible communicates a true picture of God."

OK, so let's have the' true picture' of God –
- Drum roll, please -

In His Own Words – we present – 'God':

God the sun and moon hater:

*Suppose a man or woman among you, in one of your towns that the LORD your God is giving you, has done evil in the sight of the LORD your God and has violated the covenant by serving other gods or **by worshipping the sun, the moon, or any of the forces of heaven, which I have strictly forbidden.** When you hear about it, investigate the matter thoroughly. If it is true that this detestable thing has been done in Israel, then that man or woman must be taken to the gates of the town and stoned to death.* (Deuteronomy 17:2-5 NLT)

Isn't that astonishing! The god-chap is against worship of the forces of heaven, against the sun, the moon – interesting and strange – I mean isn't God supposed to have created the sun and the moon? Without them we are very dead, aren't we?

God the jealous killer:

They entered into a covenant to seek the Lord, the God of their fathers, with all their heart and soul; and everyone who would not seek the Lord, the God of Israel, was to be put to death, whether small or great, whether man or woman. (2 Chronicles 15:12-13 NAB)

Do as you are told or be put to death!

The next one is my favorite. It really sums up the arrogant, angry, egotistical, belligerent, bullying, violent, murderous, vengeful, condemning, punishing, psychopathic monster that the nice people of the Bible Society want us to worship as our Creator.

God the genocidal egotist.

Suppose you hear in one of the towns the LORD your God is giving you that some worthless rabble among you have led their fellow citizens astray by encouraging them to worship foreign gods. In such cases, you must examine the facts carefully. If you find it is true and can prove that such a detestable act has occurred among you, you must attack that town and completely destroy all its inhabitants, as well as all the livestock. Then you must pile all the plunder in the middle of the street and burn it. **Put the entire town to the torch as a burnt offering to the LORD your God.** That town must remain a ruin forever; it may never be rebuilt. Keep none of the plunder that has been set apart for destruction. Then the LORD will turn from his fierce anger and be merciful to you. He will have compassion on you and make you a great nation, just as he solemnly promised your ancestors. "The LORD your God will be merciful only if you obey him and keep all the commands I am giving you today, doing what is pleasing to him." (Deut. 13:12-18 NWT)

If we obeyed that, there would be no towns left anywhere!

God the purger:

Anyone arrogant enough to reject the verdict of the judge or of the priest who represents the LORD your God must be put to death. Such evil must be purged from Israel. (Deut. 17:12 NLT)

Translation: Do as you are told shall be the whole of the law!

God the control freak:

The LORD then gave these further instructions to Moses: 'Tell the people of Israel to keep my Sabbath day, for the Sabbath is a sign of the covenant between me and you forever. It helps you to remember that I am the LORD, who makes you holy. Yes, keep the Sabbath day, for it is holy. Anyone who desecrates it must die; anyone who works on that day will be cut off from the community. Work six days only, but the seventh day must be a day of total rest. I repeat: Because the LORD considers it a holy day, anyone who works on the Sabbath must be put to death.' (Exodus 31:12-15 NLT)

If this still applied, there would be hardly anyone left!

God the punisher:

If one curses his father or mother, his lamp will go out at the coming of darkness. (Proverbs 20:20 NAB)

All who curse their father or mother must be put to death. They are guilty of a capital offense. (Leviticus 20:9 NLT)

Whoever strikes his father or mother shall be put to death. (Exodus 21:15 NAB)

God the murdering mysogenist:

But if this charge is true (that she wasn't a virgin on her wedding night), *and evidence of the girls virginity is not found, they shall bring the girl to the entrance of her father's house and there her townsman shall stone her to death, because she committed a crime against Israel by her unchastity in her father's house. Thus shall you purge the evil from your midst.* (Deuteronomy 22:20-21 NAB) (Also see Leviticus 21:9)

And what about men who are not virgins on their wedding night? No mention, of course!

God the killer of seers:

A man or a woman who acts as a medium or fortuneteller shall be put to death by stoning; they have no one but themselves to blame for their death. (Leviticus 20:27 NAB)

God the killer of prophets:

If a man still prophesies, his parents, father and mother, shall say to him, "You shall not live, because you have spoken a lie in the name of the Lord." When he prophesies, his parents, father and mother, shall thrust him through. (Zechariah 13:3 NAB)]

God the killer of gays:

If a man lies with a male as with a women, both of them shall be put to death for their abominable deed; they have forfeited their lives. (Leviticus 20:13 NAB)

(Note: Matthew Fox, in his Thesis 72 states: *"Since homo-sexuality is found amongst 464 species and in 8% of the human population, it is altogether natural for those who are born that way and is a gift from God and nature to the greater community."* Thesis 73 states: *"Homophobia in any form is a serious sin against love of neighbor, a sin of ignorance of the richness and diversity of God's Creation as well as a sin of exclusion."*

All three male dominated religions are homophobic and use homosexuals – a natural minority everywhere – as conven-ient scapegoats to unite their followers in bigotry. The Native American people, a more matriarchal and spiritually advanced society, and other similar pre-god-chap cultures, saw homo-sexuals as people who Creator-God had relieved of the task of parenting and therefore had a special purpose for in life.

God the child slaughterer:

*"The glory of Israel will fly away like a bird, for your children will die at birth or perish in the womb or never even be conceived. Even if your children do survive to grow up, I will take them from you. It will be a terrible day when I turn away and leave you alone. I have watched Israel become as beautiful and pleasant as Tyre. But now Israel will bring out her children to be slaughtered. "O LORD, what should I request for your people? I will ask for wombs that don't give birth and breasts that give no milk." The LORD says, "All their wickedness began at Gilgal; there I began to hate them. I will drive them from my land because of their evil actions. I will love them no more because all their leaders are rebels. The people of Israel are stricken. Their roots are dried up; they will bear no more fruit. **And***

if they give birth, I will slaughter their beloved children."
(Hosea 9:11-16 NLT)

Such a nice loving God-Chap!

God the serial killer:

Then I heard the LORD say to the other men, "Follow him through the city and kill everyone whose forehead is not marked. Show no mercy; have no pity! Kill them all — old and young, girls and women and little children. But do not touch anyone with the mark. Begin your task right here at the Temple." So they began by killing the seventy leaders. "Defile the Temple!" the LORD commanded. **"Fill its courtyards with the bodies of those you kill! Go!"** *So they went throughout the city and did as they were told.* (Ezekiel 9:5-7 NLT)

Another good example of "God's love"?

God the nation shatterer:

"You are my battle-ax and sword," says the LORD. **"With you I will shatter nations and destroy many kingdoms. With you I will shatter armies, destroying the horse and rider, the chariot and charioteer. With you I will shatter men and women, old people and children, young men and maidens. With you I will shatter shepherds and flocks, farmers and oxen, captains and rulers.** *As you watch, I will repay Babylon and the people of Babylonia for all the wrong they have done to my people in Jerusalem," says the LORD. "Look, O mighty mountain, destroyer of the earth! I am your enemy," says the LORD. "I will raise my fist against you, to roll you down from the heights. When I am finished, you will be nothing but a heap of rubble. You will be desolate forever. Even your stones will never again be used for building. You will be completely wiped out," says the LORD.* (Jeremiah 51:20-26)

(Note that after 'God' promises the Israelites a victory against Babylon, the Israelites actually lose the battle. So much for an all-knowing and all-powerful 'god'.)

God says kill, war, famine, destroy, horror:

Then the LORD said to me, "Even if Moses and Samuel stood before me pleading for these people, I wouldn't help them. Away with them! Get them out of my sight! And if they say to you, 'But where can we go?' tell them, **"This is what the LORD says: Those who are destined for death, to death; those who are destined for war, to war; those who are destined for famine, to famine; those who are destined for captivity, to captivity.** *I will send four kinds of destroyers against them," says the LORD. "I will send the sword to kill, the dogs to drag away, the vultures to devour, and the wild animals to finish up what is left. Because of the wicked things Manasseh son of Hezekiah, king of Judah, did in Jerusalem, I will make my people an object of horror to all the kingdoms of the earth."* (Jeremiah 15:1-4 NLT)

How can that possibly be God? Is it not insane to worship such a violent, vicious character?? Will some Bible basher try somehow to tell us this is an expression of 'God's love'???

God the brother, friend and neighbor killer:

(Moses) *stood at the entrance to the camp and shouted, "All of you who are on the LORD's side, come over here and join me." And all the Levites came. He told them,* **"This is what the LORD, the God of Israel, says: Strap on your swords! Go back and forth from one end of the camp to the other, killing even your brothers, friends, and neighbors."** *The Levites obeyed Moses, and about three thousand people died that day. Then Moses told the Levites, "Today you have been ordained for the service of the LORD, for you obeyed him even though it meant killing your*

57

own sons and brothers. *Because of this, he will now give you a great blessing."* (Exodus 32:26-29)

God the slaver and rapist:

God seems, if we are to seriously believe the Bible, to condone and even approve of rape.

As you approach a town to attack it, first offer its people terms for peace. If they accept your terms and open the gates to you, then all the people inside will serve you in forced labor (that means slavery), But if they refuse to make peace and prepare to fight, you must attack the town. When the LORD your God hands it over to you, kill every man in the town. But **you may keep for yourselves all the women, children,** *livestock, and other plunder.* **You may enjoy the spoils of your enemies that the LORD your God has given you.** (Deut. 20:10-14)

God the murderer and pimp:

They attacked Midian just as the LORD had commanded Moses, and they killed all the men... (On their return) Moses, Eleazar the priest, and all the leaders of the people went to meet them outside the camp. But Moses was furious with all the military commanders who had returned from the battle. "Why have you let all the women live?" he demanded. "These are the very ones who followed Balaam's advice and caused the people of Israel to rebel against the LORD at Mount Peor. They are the ones who caused the plague to strike the LORD's people. **Now kill all the boys and all the women who have slept with a man. Only the young girls who are virgins may live; you may keep them for yourselves.** (Numbers 31:7-18 NLT)

So God (through Moses) advocates killing everyone except the young, virginal women who you can keep for yourselves, fellas. This surely is quite the most 'convenient' 'god' ever invented.

(An aside about the) – **Obsession with Virginity:**

I remember when I was a teenager (1950's) there was this comic myth that all the nice girls were virgins and all the boys were experienced (no boy's ego could possible admit otherwise) so there must have been a very small number of extremely busy erotic girls. The burning question was who were they and how could we meet them?

But isn't it absurd? Look at this as food for a moment. Would a sensible man seek out a wife or partner who was a culinary virgin? Who had never entered a kitchen where food was being prepared, who was totally ignorant of the sensual effect of spices, who had no previous experience of creating mouthwatering delights of enchanting rapture, tongue tingling tastes and flavours of palate rousing pleasures, oral relishes to infatuate??

The Islamist fundamentalists apparently tell their suicide bombers that they will get seventy virgins when they get to heaven. Well, here are two thoroughly heretical thoughts:

1: Why virgins? Why not thoroughly experienced expert mistresses of eroticism who know every sensual delight?

2: Oh dear, I just don't seem to have a body any more to enjoy this….

God the human sacrificer:

In Genesis, Abraham is ordered by 'God' to sacrifice his son: *"Take your son, your only son – yes, Isaac, whom you love so much – and go to the land of Moriah. Sacrifice him there as a burnt offering on one of the mountains, which I will point out to you."* (Genesis 22:1-18)

If we take this story literally – Abraham takes his own son up on a mountain and builds an altar upon which to burn him. He even lies to his son and has him help build the altar. Then Abraham ties his son to the altar and puts a knife to his throat. He then hears 'God' tell him this was just a test of his faith. However, 'God' still wanted to smell some burnt flesh (!) so he tells Abraham to kill and burn a ram.

This is an incredibly cruel thing to do. Just think of the effect around trust on Isaac as he grows up! Imagine being a psychotherapist confronted with a life story like this! If Abraham did that today he would be in jail serving a long sentence. Some Christians somehow manage to see this story as a sign of God's 'love'.

There is another thing to think about too. This 'God-Chap' tests Abraham's 'faith' in this horrendously cruel manner. What on earth kind of a 'God' is that? Abraham passes this test of obedience to authority at the expense of his integrity, his fatherhood and the love of his son – showing himself to be a weak, malleable, pathetic individual. And he is the grandfather of male-monotheism?

Ask yourself: Would you be happy with a father like that? A father who would lie to you and then threaten to put you to death?

And just who is this cruel, domineering, capricious, unloving, manipulator of a 'God'?? And what kind of 'God' enjoys the smell of burning flesh? Something is dreadfully wrong with this story.

(With regard to obedience to authority – and Abraham's legacy in this regard – take a good look at the Milgram experiment in chapter 10.)

However, if we take the story metaphorically – *"The Bible speaks repeatedly of Abraham's faith. He believed God, we are told, and his faith was counted to him for righteousness. He represents faith in its early establishment in the consciousness, and in his life we see portrayed the different movements of the faith faculty on the various planes of human action."* From The Metaphysical Bible.

From this point of view, Isaac is an aspect of Abraham's consciousness and Abraham represents deep faith.

God and 'The Promised Land'.

Do you remember the famous myth that 'God' graciously 'gave' the Promised Land to the Israelites? Have you ever wondered about fate of the people who lived there?

From Wikipedia: Joshua *"carries out a systematic campaign against the civilians of Canaan - men, women and children - that amounts to genocide."* In doing this he is carrying out <u>herem</u> as commanded by Yahweh in Deuteronomy 20:17: *"You shall not leave alive anything that breathes."* …Joshua tells how every enemy is exterminated, thus glorifying Yahweh and promoting Israel's claim to the land.

What strange kind of a 'God' is 'glorified' by such killing? And is so completely partisan? Certainly not a 'God' for All of Us – or a 'God' of love.

God the slave lord:

If we are to believe the Bible, God supports slavery in both the Old and New Testaments. The Bible clearly approves of slavery and it goes so far as to tell how to obtain slaves, how hard you can beat them, and when you can have sex with the female slaves!

Many Jews and Christians prefer to ignore the moral problems of slavery by saying that these slaves were actually servants or indentured servants. Many translations of the Bible use the word 'servant,' 'bond servant,' or 'man servant' instead of 'slave' to make the Bible seem less immoral than it really is. While many slaves may have worked as household servants, that doesn't mean they were not slaves who were bought, sold, and treated like livestock. The following passage shows that slaves are clearly property to be bought and sold.

However, you may purchase male or female slaves from among the foreigners who live among you. You may also purchase the children of such resident foreigners, including those who have been born in your land. *You may treat them as your property,* passing them on to your children as a permanent inheritance. You may treat your slaves like this, but the people of Israel, your relatives, must never be treated this way. (Leviticus 25:44-46 NLT)

God the flogger:

When a man strikes his male or female slave with a rod so hard that the slave dies under his hand, he shall be punished. If, however, the slave survives for a day or two, he is not to be punished, since the slave is his own property. (Exodus 21:20-21 NAB)

So that must be the origin of the saying, beloved of the boys boarding school system pre 1970: 'Beaten within an inch of your life.'

Slavery approved of in the New Testament:

Slaves, obey your earthly masters with deep respect and fear. Serve them sincerely as you would serve Christ. (Ephesians 6:5 NLT)

Slaves, obey in everything those who are your earthly masters. Colossians 3:22

... bid slaves to be submissive to their masters and give satis-faction in every respect... Titus 2:9

Christians who are slaves should give their masters full respect so that the name of God and his teaching will not be shamed. If your master is a Christian, that is no excuse for being disrespectful. You should work all the harder because you are helping another believer by your efforts. Teach these truths, Timothy, and encourage everyone to obey them. (1 Timothy 6:1-2 NLT)

A God of Love? How is it so many people still, in this 21st century when we presume lots of people to be intelligent, worship at the throne of this ghastly, murderous, vengeful character?

This is not God at all, it cannot be. There has been a monstrous mistake.

It hasn't always been like this:

"War is a primary patriarchal contribution to culture, almost entirely absent form the matriarchal societies of the Neolithic and early Bronze ages. Even when Goddess-worshipping was beginning to give way to cults of aggressive gods, for a long time the appearance of the Goddess imposed peace on all hostile groups. Among Germanic Tribes in Europe, Tacitus said, whenever the Goddess moved in her chariot at certain seasons to certain sacred places, the people 'do not go to battle or wear arms; every weapon is under lock; peace and quiet are known and welcomed'.... Patriarchal gods tended to be warlike from their inception – including, or even particularly the Judeo-Christian God.... Christianity was never a pacifist religion... all-male Christianity was disseminated by violence."

— Barbara G. Walker, *Womens Encyclopedia* (p1058)

That is a little of the Old Testament. There is lots more like it which you can research for yourself if you need convincing of its incredible murderous bloodthirstyness.

Some say - well the Old Testament may be full of blood and guts but the New Testament is all about love and peace. Oh yea? Really? Are you sure? Have you read it intelligently? Questioned it? Let's take a look:-

New Testament:

Here is a question for you. Which well known New Testament personage said this?

These enemies of mine who did not want me to be **king over them** *– bring them here* **and kill them in front of me.**

OR from another translation:- *'But those mine enemies, which would not that I should reign over them, bring hither, and slay them before me.* (Luke 19:27)

Now this passage comes right at the end of the parable of the nobleman's slaves who are blessed for capitalism (turning one pound into ten) and cursed for being careful (keeping one pound safe). It ends with the decree: *'Take from him the pound and give to him who hath ten pounds.'*

Very strange kind of parable, when you consider it means *'Blessed be the speculators'*! (This may not be the only way of interpreting this parable, but it is one of them.)

Then verse 26, 27 & 28 follow:

26: *For I say unto you. That unto everyone which hath shall be given; and from him that hath not, even that which he hath shall be taken away from him.*

27: **Moreover, these enemies of mine who did not want me to be king over them – bring them here and kill them in front of me.**

28: *So when he had said these things, he began to go on ahead, going up to Jerusalem.*

Amazing, huh? Never mentioned in church! Never taught in Sunday School. Gentle Jesus not so gentle after all. However that statement fits very well with the following ones:

If any man come unto me, and hate not his father, and mother, and wife, and children, and brother, and sisters, yea, and his own soul also, he cannot be my disciple. Whoever is not carrying his torture stake and coming after me cannot be my disciple. Luke 14:26-27,

But whosoever shall deny me before men, him I will also deny before my Father which is in heaven. Think not I am come to send peace on earth: I came not to send peace, but rather a sword.

For I am come to set a man at variance against his father, and the daughter against her mother and the daughter-in-law against her mother-in-law

If you love your father, mother, sister, brother, more than me, you are not worthy of being mine. Matthew 10:33-37

...and he that hath no sword, let him sell his garment, and buy one. Luke 22.36.

And every one that hath forsaken houses, or brethren, or sisters, or father, or mother, or wife, or children, or lands, for my name's sake, shall receive an hundredfold, and shall inherit everlasting life." Mark 10.29-30.

Do not think I came to destroy the Law and the Prophets. I came not to destroy but to fulfill. Matthew 5:17

Brother shall deliver up the brother to death, and the father the child: and the children shall rise up against their parents, and cause them to be put to death. Matthew 10:21

Happy families!

He that believeth and is baptized shall be saved; but he that believeth not shall be damned. Mark 16:16.

No messing, no choice, just believe as you're told and don't dare to think, to question or have any mind, any rights or personal sovereignty of your own.

These statements are all attributed to Jesus and they sound like the words of a warlord, not a great spiritual master. This is so far from the official story of Jesus. How come? How come no one quotes the above? It is as if these statements are hidden in plain sight. Jesus the warlord, right there in the Gospels, and hardly anyone notices. The nice people of the Bible Society would be quite shocked, I'm sure, to realise that these statements are all there right under their noses.

By contrast in Matthew 15:4, he says: *God said "Honor thy mother and father. Let him that reviles father or mother end up in death".*

Either way you end up in the sh*t – if you don't honor them he wants you to you die and if you don't hate them you cannot be a disciple!

So Jesus approves of the Old Testament law and the prophets? According to this, he apparently supports the incredible cruelties of the Old Testament God such as those listed in the last chapter. Not what I was taught in Sunday school. How come the teachers left all that out?

St Paul too supports the bloodthirsty Old Testament laws:

"Any man that has disregarded the Law of Moses dies without compassion upon the testimony of two or three." (Paul in Hebrews 10:28)

So it just takes two or three to rat on one person and they end up dead? Hebrews 10:29 is interesting too – take a look - but let us go on to 10:30-31:

*For we know him that said "Vengeance is mine: I will recompense," and again: "Jehovah will judge his people. **It is a fearful thing to fall into the hands of the living God.***"

And again: "... I the Lord thy God am a **jealous God,** visiting the iniquity of the fathers upon the children unto the third and fourth generation." - Exodus 20:5*

Oh my God, I say - - Save us - - from god!

Jesus also makes many quite different and opposing statements to the above such as the familiar ones that Bible teachers teach you. Take a look at these:

Matthew 26:52: *"Put up again thy sword into his place: for all that take the sword shall perish with the sword".*

"Turn the other cheek," do not react to violence with violence.

*"Behold, the kingdom of heaven is **within you."***

So God is within, not outside you, and by implication, in the world, not outside it. This is the understanding of the animists and the heathens – God is in the heath, in nature. And nature includes people, animals, plants, insects – everything on earth and the earth herself.

Here are some of Jesus' very confused and convoluted statements on judgment:

"For the Father judgeth no man, but hath committed all judgment unto the Son." – John 5.22.

And Jesus said, *"For judgment I am come into this world."* – John 9.39.

"I judge no man." – John 8.15.

"I came not to judge the world, but to save the world." – John 12.47.

"Judge not, and ye shall not be judged." – Luke 6.37.

When you put together Jesus's teachings like this, is it not an understatement to say they are the teachings of a rather schitzophrenic individual? I have come to the conclusion it is because there are: -

Two Different Jesus's:

1. – The Living War Leader who fought the Romans. (A 'messiah/savior' in those days meant someone who will save the Israelites from oppressors)

2. – The Mythical God-Man of the Gospels who is based on much earlier Sun-God stories/myths. (Discussed in the next chapter)

It seems to me that these two have been deeply confused. Here I want to point you to the books of Ralph Ellis who has researched ancient records very deeply. He has come up with the proposition that the physical Jesus might well be Jesus of Gamala, King of Judea who ruled, with his queen, Mary of Magdala, around the time of AD 50/70. In AD70 he was a leader of the Jewish Revolt and was caught by the Romans and crucified but taken down early and survived. There are other theories too about just who Jesus was and was not.

One strange thing is certain – the Jesus of the Gospels was so <u>un</u>important in his time that he does not appear in the historical records of the day. (Except for obvious forgeries added much later.) There may well have been a rabbi Yeshua (Jesus is the name in Greek) who taught at this time. He just didn't make it into the history books.

And now this most interesting of all the statements attributed to Jesus: *"Verily, verily, I say unto you, He that believeth in me, the works that I do shall he also; and greater works than these shall he do."*

Another translation says it fractionally differently: *"Most truly I say to you. He that exercises faith in me, that one will also do the works that I do; and he will do works greater than these, because I am going my way to the father."* (John 14:12)

This says if you exercise faith in Jesus / believe in Jesus, then you – or I – will be able to do what he can and even greater works than his, 'miracles' and all. That completely contradicts any idea that Jesus is super-special. He is saying that we can all achieve the same as him. How? By exercising faith in him or by believing in him. Just what does this really mean?

If you understand that the mythical Jesus represents the *eternal god-wo/man* within all of us, it makes complete sense. Whereas if you say you have to believe in just the one person who supposedly lived at one time and place around 2,000 years ago, and every other religion and spiritual path is wrong and useless, (and everyone who lived before Jesus and who couldn't believe in him because he didn't exist is therefore left in 'limbo') you end up struggling with very crazy upside-down scriptures to 'prove' your case.

Here is a whole different way of looking at this. From The Metaphysical Bible:

Jesus represents God's idea of man in expression: Christ is that idea in absolute. Jesus Christ was the type man, which includes all the mental phases through which man passes in demonstrating life's problems. So we find JC passing through all the trials, temptations, and mental variations of each of us, "yet without sin" that is, not falling under the dominion of evil thoughts. The experiences of each individual are in miniature the experiences of all.

Jesus in the temple, at the age of twelve years, represents the growing consciousness within us that we are sons (& daughters) of God (Luke 2:40-52)

Jesus going about all the cities and villages, teaching, preaching, and healing, represents the I AM in its universal capacity as a teacher and harmonizer of its own mental and bodily conditions (Matt 9:35)

The twelve sent forth by Jesus (Matt 10:5) typify the twelve facul-ties of mind in every man, functioning under the direction of I AM.

The I (Jesus) and His disciples (faculties) are always hidden to these unions of planes of consciousness (Marriages; -see John 2:2)

Jesus in Luke 7: 36-38 represents Divine Mind in its search for the motive rather than the outer act.

The temptation of Jesus (Matt 4:1-11) took place within himself. The place of overcoming is within the consciousness of man. When we follow Jesus we rise above the demands of the flesh-and-sense world. The forty days' fast is an all-round denial of sense demands. In fasting, we in our thoughts, live above the material needs. We are "led up", and our appetites and passions are for a season in such an eclipse that we think that they will trouble no more. But "he after-ward hungered". There is a return to sense consciousness.

The devil is personality, the adverse consciousness that has been built up in ignorance and disregard of the divine law. To worship the devil is to worship personality; to live in personal consciousness and give it the substance of our life and thought.

The Real God – Infinite Creator – is All-That-Is and creates out of Its Self (which is All-That-Is) – all dimensions, all galaxies, all stars, all planets, all beings, all humans, all everything....

We are all sons and daughters of Creation.

The Son of God is the Sun and the Virgin Mary (Mare) is the oceans of Mother Earth from which life is birthed.

We all come from the Goddess
And to her we shall return
Like a drop of rain,
Flowing to the ocean

Chapter 5
The Many God-Men before Jesus

Did they tell you Jesus is the ONLY son of God? Did you believe them? Do you still?

Well, prepare for a surprise. Jesus is not the only son of God at all. There are loads more and they all pre-date Jesus. He is the last one – and most importantly – he is the only one who has been taken literally as a live corporeal human being. All the others were, and are, understood to be mythological beings.

Justin Martyr, in his *First Apology, 21* says:

"When we say that the Word, who is the first-birth of God, was produced without sexual union, and that He, Jesus Christ, our Teacher, was crucified and died, and rose again, and ascended into heaven, we propounded nothing different from what you believe regarding those whom you esteem sons of Jupiter"

In other words, the same in essence as the Pagan beliefs before Christianity.

One thing is certain – far from being the first, Jesus was the last of a long line of God-Men and his story had been told many times before in many cultures.

Consider **Horus**. Heard Of him? No? Well, take a look at his story and see if you recognize it.

- Horus was the "only begotten son of God." In this case, God was called Osiris.

- Horus's mother was Isis-MERI. Jesus' mother was MARY.

- The foster father of Horus was Seb.

- The foster father of Jesus was Joseph. Both of them were of 'royal descent.'

- Isis-Meri conceived Horus without the "seed of the living father." Osiris was both *dead* and had no penis, so Isis-Meri made a dildo out of clay. Mary conceived Jesus without the seed of a living father.

- Horus was born "In a cave." Jesus was born "in a cave or stable."

- Horus was heralded by the Star "Sirius" and witnessed by "3 solar deities." Jesus was heralded by "a Star in the East". Sirius just so happens to be the brightest star in the East that rises at dawn. The "Three Wise men" are the 3 stars on Orion's Belt. The title of these 3 stars for thousands of years was "The Three Kings of Orion".

- Horus's birth date was at the time of the winter solstice (December 21-22) with December 25 being the date the SUN begins to 'rise again' as it is the first day that is measurably longer. Jesus Birth date is recognized as December 25. This date is the same date as the birthday of Mithras, Dionysus and the Sol Invictus (unconquerable Sun), and many other God-men of ancient mythology.

- Herut tried to have Horus murdered. Herod tried to have Jesus murdered.

- God tells Horus' mother, "Come, thou goddess Isis-Meri, hide thyself with thy child." An angel tells Jesus' father to: "Arise and take the young child and his mother and flee into Egypt."

- Horus came of age (12) with a special ritual when his eye was restored. Jesus was taken by parents to the temple for what is today called a Bar Mitzvah ritual, his age? 12. This is when they both "came of age."

- Jesus reputedly challenged the elders of the temple at this age. Just as every adolescent challenges the status quo!

- Between the ages of 12-30 there is nothing written about either Horus or Jesus.

- Horus was baptized in the river Eridanus. There is a Constellation called Eridanus that looks like a river in the sky. Jesus was baptized in the river Jordan.

- Horus was baptized by "Anup the baptizer." Jesus was baptized by "John the Baptist." Both baptizers were beheaded.

- Jesus & Horus went through temptations at the same period in their lives. Horus was taken from the desert of Amenta up a high mountain by his arch-rival Sut. (Sut or Set-An was a precursor for the Hebrew Satan.) Jesus was taken from the desert in Palestine up a high mountain by his arch-rival Satan.

- Horus walked on water, cast out demons, healed the sick, restored sight to the blind. He "stilled the sea by his power." Jesus walked on water, cast out demons, healed the sick, restored sight to the blind. He stilled the sea with the command "Peace, be still".

- The place of resurrection for Horus was Anu, an Egyptian city where the rites of the death, burial and resurrection of Horus were enacted annually. The place of resurrection for Jesus was Bethany. Hebrews added their prefix for house ('beth") to "Anu" to produce "Beth-Anu" or the "House of Anu." Since "u" and "y" were interchangeable in antiquity, "Bethanu" became "Bethany."

- Horus raised "Asar" from the dead. He was referred to as "The Asar," as a sign of respect. Translated into Hebrew, this is "El-Asar." The Romans added the suffix "us" to indicate a male name, producing "Elasarus." Over time, the "E" was dropped and "s" became "z," producing "Lazarus."

- Horus was "the Lamb." Jesus was "the Lamb."

- Horus was the way, the truth and the life, by name and in person. Jesus was the way, the truth and the life.

- Horus is the Good Shepherd with the crook upon his shoulders. Jesus is the Good Shepherd with the lamb upon his shoulders.

- Horus and Jesus both had 12 Disciples. Once we drop the literalist myth, we can dare to realize these are SUN of God myths, we can see that the disciples are the 12 houses of the zodiac.

And by the way, the Horus story dates back perhaps as much as three thousand years before Jesus. The very idea that Jesus is the literal 'only son of God' and that his story is in any way unique is ridiculous and easily challenged through a proper in-depth look at available historical information. No wonder there are so many injunctions for Christians to read nothing but the Bible – they might learn too much to remain Christians!

There are many such *God-men, saviors, Messiahs, Sons of God,* all of whom come before Jesus. Here are a few more:

*"The worship of **Attis** and Cybele dates back centuries in Phrygia (modern Turkey) and it was imported to Rome in 204 BC. Roman*

writers mentioning the religion include: Lucretius (98 - 54 BC), Catullus (86 - 40 BC), Varro (116 - 28 BC), and Dionysus Halicarnasensis (first century BC). The 'Festival of Joy' which celebrated Attis' death and rebirth was a yearly event in Rome before and during the years the Christian Gospels were written (from the reign of Claudius, 41 - 54 AD).

"On March 22 a pine tree was brought to the sanctuary of Cybele, on it hung the effigy of Attis. The God was dead. Two days of mourning followed, but when night fell on the eve of the third day, the worshippers turned to joy. 'For suddenly a light shone in the darkness; the tomb was opened; the God had risen from the dead ... [and the priest] softly whispered in their ears the glad tidings of salvation. The resurrection of the God was hailed by his disciples as a promise that they too would issue triumphant from the corruption of the grave.'"

— Frazer, *Attis*, chapter 1

The worshippers of Attis then ate a sacramental meal of bread and wine. The wine represented the God's blood; the bread became the body of the savior.

Baptism was a serious ceremony: a bull was placed over a grating and the devotee stood under the grating. The bull was then stabbed with a consecrated spear and, *"Its hot reeking blood poured in torrents through the apertures and was received with devout eagerness by the worshipper ... who had been born again to eternal life and had washed away his sins in the blood of the bull."*

Heavy duty when you compare it with modern day church wine and biscuit!

The basics of the Attis story were:

- He was born of the virgin Nana on December 25th
- He was both the divine father and the divine son.

- He was a savior who was crucified in a tree for the salvation of mankind and was buried, but on the third day the priests found the tomb empty as he had arisen from the dead. The date was March 25.

- His followers were baptized in blood, thereby washing away their sins, after which they were declared 'born again.'

- His followers ate a sacred meal of bread which they believed became the body of the savior.

- At the spring solstice celebration he is depicted hanging on a tree.

- He is called 'The Good Shepherd,' the 'Most High God,' the 'Only Begotten Son,' and the 'Savior.'

Here is **Mithras**, another God-man myth from Persia:

- Mithras was born in a cave, on December 25, of a virgin mother. He came from heaven to be born as a man, to redeem men from their sin. He was known as "Savior," "Son of God," "Redeemer," and "Lamb of God."

- Every year at the first minute of December 25, the temple of Mithras was lit with candles and priests in white garments **celebrated the birth of the Son of God.**

- His followers kept the Sabbath holy, eating sacramental meals in remembrance of Him. The sacred meal of bread and water, or bread and wine, was symbolic of the body and blood of the sacred bull.

- Mithraic rituals were to bring about the transformation and salvation of His adherents – the ascent of the soul to the realm of the divine. On the wall of a Mithraic temple in Rome is the inscription: "And thou hast saved us by shedding the eternal blood."

- The great Mithraic festivals celebrated his birth (at the winter solstice) and his death and resurrection (at the spring solstice).

The devil's mimicry!

A Christian writer of the fourth century AD recounted ongoing disputes between Pagans and Christians over the remarkable similarities of the death and resurrection of their gods. The Pagans argued that their Gods were older and therefore original. The Christians admitted Christ came later, but claimed Attis / Mithras etc were the work of the devil and their similarity to Christ, and the fact they predated Christ, were intended to confuse and mislead men!

Now isn't that just great. But there is one problem – well a lot really, but let us just look at one. If the 'Devil' is so clever as to create the Jesus story long before 'God', doesn't that make the 'Devil' seriously prescient and 'God' a bit of a dimwit?

Here is a recent Creationist Christian creating a wonderful story, Monty Pythonesque in its fabulous implausibility. He says that before the Great Flood and the time of Noah, there were good and bad angels/demons who had come down to earth in disobedience of God and that when the flood wiped out almost all mankind, it didn't kill the bad angels and so they lived for many years without people around to see what they got up to. So during that time, Satan, their leader got them to make up fake fossils and dinosaur bones and bury them all over the place to trick later generations of people into thinking history was longer than what the church and the good Bishop Ussher decreed.

Well, you have to give the fool credit for sheer creative invention!

Let us look at some more of the many God-Men who preceded Jesus and carried the same myth, starting with **Buddha**:

- He was born of the Virgin **Maya (!)** on December 25, announced by a star and attended by wise men presenting costly gifts. At his birth angels sang heavenly songs.

- His parents fleed with him to another land to escape an infanticide ordered by King Bimbasara.

- He taught in temple at age 12 and amazed the priests with his knowledge.

- He was tempted by Mara, the Evil One, while fasting.

- He was baptized in water with the Spirit of God present.

- He healed the sick, fed 500 from a small basket of cakes, walked on water.

- He came to fulfill the law and preached the establishment of a kingdom of righteousness.

- He taught that his followers should renounce the world and embrace a life of poverty.

- He was transfigured on a mount.

- He died (on a cross, in some traditions), was buried but rose again after the tomb was opened by supernatural powers.

- He ascended into heaven (Nirvana) and will return in later days to judge the dead.

- He was called: "Good Shepherd," "Carpenter," "Alpha and Omega," "Sin Bearer," "Master," "Light of the World," "Redeemer," etc.

Notice anything similar?

There have been many Buddhas over the centuries up to the last one about 2,500 years ago. I do not see them as being any more corporeal than Jesus or any of the other God-men.

Here is **Dionysos**, also known as **Bacchus**, the Greek version of the myth. The essence of the Dionysos story is:

- Born of a virgin on December 25 and placed in a manger.
- He became a traveling teacher and performed many miracles.
- He rode in a triumphal procession on an ass.
- He turned water into wine.
- His followers ate a sacred meal that became the body of the God.
- He rose from the dead on March 25.
- He was identified with the ram and the lamb.
- Called "King of Kings," "Only Begotten Son," "Savior," "Redeemer," "Sin bearer," "Anointed One," the "Alpha and Omega."

And another! This is the story of **Virishna**, a heathen savior said to date back to 1200 BC.

Incidentally, do you know the meaning of *heathen*, so derided by Christians? A heathen (me) is one *who sees God in the heath*, i.e., in nature, in everything. And where else would you look? If God is not in the substance of life, of existence – and the very substance of life/existence in God – then where is S/He?

Virishna was immaculately conceived and born of a spotless virgin who had 'never known man' and who was impregnated by a spirit. Angels and shepherds attended his birth offering frankincense and myrrh. His birth occurred according to a prophecy; he was threatened in early life by the local tyrant Cansa and his parents fled with him to Gokul. All the male children under two were then murdered by Cansa. He was saluted and worshipped as the 'savior of men'; he led a life of humility and service, wrought astounding miracles including healing the sick, restoring sight to the blind, casting out devils, raising the dead, etc. He was put to death on a cross between two thieves. He descended to hell, rose from the dead and ascended up to heaven 'in the sight of all men.'

You can't get much closer to the Jesus story than that!

There are an awful lot of God-Men in mythology and here is a partial list, courtesy of *The Book Your Church Does Not Want You to Read.* (But please do! p.135):

- Krishna of Hindostan

- Buddha Sakia of India

- Salivahana of Bermuda

- Osiris of Egypt

- Horus of Egypt

- Odin of Scandinavia

- Crite of Chaldea

- Zoroaster of Persia

- Mithra – also Persia

- Baal and Taut of Phoenicia

- Indra of Tibet
- Bali of Afghanistan
- Jao of Nepal
- Virishna of India
- Wittoba of the Bilingonese
- Thammuz of Syria
- Attis of Phrigia
- Xamolxis of Thrace
- Zoar of the Bonzes
- Adad of Assyria
- Deva Tat and Sammonocadam of Siam
- Alcides of Thebes
- Mikado of the Sintoos
- Beddru of Japan
- Hesus or Eros, and Bremrillah of the Druids
- Thor, son of Odin, of the Gauls
- Cadmus of Greece
- Dionysos, also Greece
- Adonis, son of the virgin Io of Greece
- Hil and Feta of the Mandaites
- Quetzalcoatl of Mexico. Also Gentaut.
- Prometheus of Caucasus
- Ischy of Formosa
- Fohi and Tien of China
- Ixion nd Quirinus of Rome

One particular story about the origin of 'Jesus Christ'
is told by Australian writer Tony Bushby. He says that at the
Council of Nicaea, Emperor Constantine wanted a new and
all encompassing god-man and so he was named by taking a
Druid God from Constantine's country (Britain) to suit the
Western Church and please the emperor, put together with
an Eastern God to pacify the Eastern Church. The Druid was
called Hesus and the eastern God was Krishna so the new god
became Hesus-Krishna. Krishna is Christos in latin and there
was no J sound till much later (9th century or so) so Hesus
Krishna became Jesus Christos = Jesus Christ! I don't know if
there's truth in that, but in the mire of history there certainly
could be.

Some say the myth of the dying-reborn god probably
started in Asia Minor, although it could well be more universal
because we find it in Mexico in the myth of Quetzalcoatl and
as far east as China. The ancient Greeks and Romans inherited
and adapted gods from places like Assyria, Babylon, Phrygia,
Persia, Mesopotamia and Egypt. The ancient religions were
about the cycles of the Sun (the Sun of God) and the Earth
(The Divine Mother) and the cycles of nature. They saw the
great forces of the Universe as 'gods' who personified nature's
cycles by dying in the winter and being reborn in the spring.

From writer/researcher Neil Cramer – The Cleaver,
January 2011:

"*Equating Mithra with Jesus was a straightforward piece of
politico-religious propaganda. Basically, Emperor Aurelian merged
major Roman festivals of Saturnalia (the festival of Saturn) and Sol
Invictus with a number of celebrations of other gods and saviours
from other religions into a single special day, the 25th December.
Following various theological deliberations, the emergent Christian
edifice agreed to adopt this date as the birthday of their savior too,
Jesus Christ. As many of the lands that Rome was seeking to absorb*

were already accustomed to their own festivals on or around 25th December, it was easy for Roman spin-masters to switch people's focus onto the new son on the block – Jesus."

All the evidence shows quite conclusively that a gigantic fraud of monumental proportions had been perpetrated upon us. 'Jesus Christ' is a story, a mythological personage, and never was a person. Here is Archarya S writing in *The Christ Conspiracy*:

"The fact is that this crowd-drawing preacher finds his place in 'history' only in the New Testament, **completely overlooked by the dozens of historians of his day, an era considered one of the best documented in history**."

And Albert Schweitzer in his book *The Quest for the Historical Jesus* wrote:

"There is nothing more negative than the result of the critical study of the life of Jesus ... it has fallen to pieces, cleft and disintegrated by the concrete historical problems which came to the surface one after another." (Quoted in *The Laughing Jesus* by Timothy Freke and Peter Gandy, p.60.)

In nature, nothing is individually perfect. The Yin is never completely yin and the yang never completely yang. The concept of a perfect savior is at odds with nature, with Creation, with God. A perfect savior who will come and save us is a childish idea, as is God as a Big-Daddy-in-the-Sky. When we grow up into adults we need to give up such childish concepts.

Growing up is about taking responsibility and that means becoming our own savior. No one is going to come and 'save' us from our own stupidity, ignorance and self-indulgence, we are the ones whose job it is and we are here to learn that and put it into practice.

We are here to grow up and create our-self into a being of self-mastery and self-knowledge.

Chapter 6
Origins of Christianity. One True Religion?

Do you believe that Christianity is a 'pure' religion created from a unique God-given set of principles?

Have you ever wondered about its true origins and how come so much bloodshed occurred in its early formation?

Have you ever looked into the historical record of those days?

If not, you may be in for a surprise or two as we examine some of the early politics that took place. Christianity as we know it was founded by the Emperor Constantine and became effectively formalized into an arm of the Roman state in AD325 at the Council of Nicaea. Important to note that many of the original Christians were branded as heretics by this time.

Flavius Valerius Constantius (c.285-337 AD), Constantine the Great, was the son of Emperor Constantius I. When his father died in 306 AD, Constantine became emperor of Britain, Gaul (now France), and Spain. Gradually he gained control of the entire Roman Empire.

It is said that in 312 AD, Constantine responded to a dream by converting from Paganism to Christianity so that, all of a sudden, it was good to be Christian and bad to be a Pagan. Within a century of Constantine's 'conversion', the Empire went from roughly ten percent Christian (most of these believing in now extinct "heretical" Christianities) to mostly Roman Christian. How did the conversion happen? Partly by giving Christians preference for government contracts and advancement. (Sounds familiar!) Also by some serious coercion.

Constantine made divination in public matters punishable by burning to death. Pagan sacrifices were banned in 341 AD, and nocturnal pagan worship was forbidden in 353 AD. By mid-century, pagan temples were ordered closed, and in 356 AD, worship of non-Christian images became a capital crime.

(Thanks to POCM - Pagan Origins of the Christ Myth – see http://www.medmalexperts.com/POCM/index.html   And - http://www.jesusneverexisted.com/egypt.htm)

Theological differences regarding just who Jesus Christ was began to manifest in Constantine's empire when two major opponents surfaced and argued virulently whether Jesus Christ was a created being (Arius doctrine) or not created but rather co-equal and co-eternal to God his father (Athanasius doctrine).

The theological warfare between the Arius and Athanasius camps became intense. Constantine realized that his empire was being threatened by this doctrinal rift and pressured the church to sort out its differences before the results created a massive split. Finally the emperor called the council at Nicaea in 325 AD to resolve the dispute.

Only a fraction of existing bishops, 318, attended. This equated to about 18% of all the bishops in the empire. Of the 318, approximately 10 were from the Western part of Constantine's empire, making the voting lopsided at best. The emperor manipulated, coerced and threatened the council to be sure it voted for what he wanted.

The present day Christian Church calls Constantine the first Christian emperor; however, his 'Christianity' was nothing but politically motivated. He had been a disciple of Mithras, the earlier Middle-Eastern 'god-man' from Persia. Whether he ever personally accepted Christian doctrine is more than doubtful. He had one of his sons murdered in addition to a nephew, his brother in law and probably one of his wives – not exactly ideal Christian behavior. Apparently he continued to retain his title of high priest in the Mithraic religion until his death and was not baptized into Christianity until he was on his deathbed.

The majority of bishops voted under pressure from Constantine for the Athanasius doctrine, so a creed was adopted that favored Athanasius' theology and Arius was condemned and exiled. Several of the bishops left before the voting to avoid the controversy. Jesus Christ was approved to be "one substance" with God the Father. It is interesting that, even today, the Eastern and Western Orthodox churches disagree with each other regarding this doctrine.

Two of the bishops who voted pro-Arius were also exiled and Arius' writings were destroyed. Constantine decreed that anyone caught with Arius documents would be subject to the death penalty. A good loving Christian response? Well, it would fit with the Inquisition a thousand years later, but it is not really quite the idea supposedly promoted by Jesus. But it is very typical of emperors and Church power brokers.

Here is the Nicene Creed as formulated by the Athanasius teachings

We believe in one God, the Father, the Almighty,

maker of heaven and earth, of all that is, seen and unseen.

We believe in one Lord, Jesus Christ, the only Son of God, eternally begotten of the Father,

God from God, Light from Light, true God from true God, begotten, not made, of one Being with the Father; through him all things were made.

For us and for our salvation he came down from heaven, was incarnate of the Holy Spirit and the Virgin Mary and became truly human.

For our sake he was crucified under Pontius Pilate; he suffered death and was buried.

On the third day he rose again in accordance with the Scriptures; he ascended into heaven and is seated at the right hand of the Father.

He will come again in glory to judge the living and the dead, and his kingdom will have no end.

We believe in the Holy Spirit, the Lord, the giver of life,

who proceeds from the Father and the Son, who with the Father and the Son is worshiped and glorified, who has spoken through the prophets.

We believe in one holy catholic and apostolic Church.

We acknowledge one baptism for the forgiveness of sins.

We look for the resurrection of the dead, and the life of the world to come. Amen.

Well, there's no messing about what we are all supposed to believe. Especially in one Holy Apostolic Church – no messing where the power is intended to lie. It's worth remembering that disagreeing with an emperor (or his appointed church) is a dodgy business. You can ever so easily find all your worldly goods and even your life forfeit, so the pressure to agree, whatever you might privately think, is seriously heavy.

Today we call that *mind control* or *totalitarianism*.

Even with the adoption of the Nicaean Creed, it seems that problems continued and after a few years, the Arian faction began to regain control. In fact, they became so powerful that Constantine restored them and denounced the Athanasius group. Well, it seems public pressure did impress the emperor and he bent to their power – and annexed it to his. He ended Arius' exile along with the bishops who sided with him. And now he banished Athanasius and his followers.

When Constantine died, after being baptized by an Arian Bishop, his son fully reinstated the Arian philosophy and bishops and enforced condemnation of the Athanasius group. In the following years, the political foes continued to struggle until finally the Arians were overthrown and Athanasius reinstated! Up, down and roundabout – and this is 'one true religion'? This controversy caused widespread bloodshed and killing. As ever.

In 381 AD, Emperor Theodosius who favored the Trinitarian ideas of Athanasius convened a council in Constantinople. Only Trinitarian believing bishops were invited to attend. 150 bishops attended and voted to alter the Nicene Creed to include the Holy Spirit as a part of the Godhead. The Trinity doctrine then became official for both the church and the state. Dissident bishops were expelled from the church and excommunicated. Same old jazz – never mind actual beliefs or convictions, just watch out or you'll suddenly find the wind blowing the other way with you on the wrong side.

The Athanasius Trinitarian Creed was not finally established until the 5th century. It was not written by Athanasius but adopted his name. It stated in part:

"We worship one God in Trinity . . . The Father is God, the Son is God, and the Holy Ghost is God; and yet they are not three gods, but one God."

I guess they weren't too good at mathematics. $1 + 1 + 1 = 1$. They also didn't care a jot for balance as they totally left out the Mother, the feminine and woman.

By the 9th century, the creed was established in Spain, France and Germany. It had taken centuries for the trinity doctrine to be accepted, and I wonder how much coercion, political pressure and threats it took. It was only because of church and government politics that the trinity came into existence at all and became church orthodoxy.

Here is the current version of the creed as mainly in use today:

I believe in God, the Father Almighty,
the Creator of heaven and earth,
and in Jesus Christ, His only Son, our Lord:
Who was conceived of the Holy Spirit,
born of the Virgin Mary,
suffered under Pontius Pilate,
was crucified, died, and was buried.

He descended into hell.
The third day He arose again from the dead.
He ascended into heaven
and sits at the right hand of God the Father Almighty,
whence He shall come to judge the living and the dead.

I believe in the Holy Spirit, the holy catholic church,
the communion of saints,
the forgiveness of sins, the resurrection of the body,
and life everlasting.
Amen.

It is good to remember that this doctrine came from deceit, underhanded politics, a power hungry emperor and warring factions who brought about death and bloodshed to each other. Oh, and in 391, Theodosius outlawed all religions except Christianity. So much for choice.

Another false claim of the church is the doctrine of Apostolic Succession. The Church is known to have copied this idea from a Gnostic sect in the fourth century, and then fabricated lines of apostolic succession for the missing centuries.

Very clever when you consider that the apostles they purport to succeed didn't exist anyway.

It is said by some that Christianity brought new ideals. But brotherly love and compassion had been taught by the Stoics for centuries. Love your neighbor and respect for others is found abundantly in Paganism.

"The Christian faith was a vulgarised paganism, set to the theme of the Jewish prophets and debased by religious intolerance. The early Christian sects attacked each other as energetically as they attacked pagans. 1st century Palestine had rabbis, radicals and rebels in abundance. But a 'life' conjured up from mystical fantasy, a mass of borrowed quotations, copied story elements and a corpus of self-serving speculation, does not constitute historical reality. The final defeat of militant Jewish nationalism and the eradication of the Jewish kingdom gave the incipient Christian churches the final uplift they required."

So much for 'one true religion' and 'one true church'.

(If it's not enough for you, read: *The Christ Conspiracy / The Dark Side of Christian history / The Jesus Mysteries / Jesus and the (lost) Goddess / The Laughing Jesus / The Woman's Encyclopedia of Myths and Secrets*. See Resources at the end of this book.)

And this about the cherished Biblical history of the Jews:

"Despite the mass of contemporary records that have been unearthed in Egypt, not one historical reference to the presence of the Israelites has yet been found there. Not a single mention of Joseph, the Pharaoh's 'Grand Vizier'. Not a word about Moses, or the spectacular flight from Egypt and the destruction of the pursuing Egyptian army."

From Magnus Magnusson, *The Archaeology of the Bible Lands - BC*, p43.

Also see Ralph Ellis – '*King Jesus: From Kam (Egypt) To Camelot*'. And –'*Christianity, An Ancient Egyptian Religion*' by Ahmed Osman. (Details in Resources)

Talking of 'one true...', here in Britain over the last thirty or more years, a number of high profile public figures have converted to Catholicism in their later years to join the 'one true church' before its too late. Pity they didn't take the trouble to look into real history instead of swallowing the party line. Or am I just being sarcastic? Well, maybe, but just look at this:

Question: What would a masculine, dominant, patriarchal 'God-Chap' demand to keep your allegiance, no matter what messes he makes and how cleverly the 'devil-chap' p*sses on his plans? What else but –

Your blind, unthinking faith!

Well, he would, wouldn't he?

Tertullian says:

"*We want no curious disputation after possessing Christ Jesus, no inquisition after enjoying the gospel! With our faith, we desire no further belief.*

"*This rule ... was taught by Christ, and raises amongst ourselves no other questions than those which heresies introduce, and which make men heretics.*"

And he adds: "*Credo quia incredibilis est,*" or in English: "*I believe because it is unbelievable.*"

And this: "… I maintain that the Son of God was born; why am I not ashamed of maintaining such a thing? Why! But because it is itself a shameful thing. I maintain that the son of God died: well that is wholly credible because it is monstrously absurd. I maintain that after having been buried, he rose again: and that I take to be absolutely true, because it was manifestly impossible!"

—Quoted by Rudolf Steiner in *Christianity as Mystical Fact* (Anthroposophic Press, 1972)

Well, that is what Tertullian said. Make of it what you will. I'd recommend him a long series of appointments with a really patient psychotherapist!

St. Augustine, quoted from Archarya S (p.24) said:

"I should not believe in the truth of the Gospels unless the authority of the Catholic Church forced me to do so."

Quite a statement! She says he had already accepted '*as historic truth the fabulous founding of Rome by Romulus and Remus, their virgin-birth by the god Mars, and their nursing by the she-wolf…*'

The 2nd century Epicurian philosopher Celsus, who in common with most of the Greeks, looked upon Christianity as a '*blind faith that shunned the light of reason,*' said of the Christians:

"They are forever repeating: '*Do not examine. Only believe, and thy faith will make the blessed. Wisdom is a bad thing in life; foolishness is to be preferred.*'"

Bishop Irenaeus of Lyons said:

"It is incumbent to obey the priests who are in the church (well, that is the whole point, isn't it – church control of everything including thinking.) … those who possess the succession from the apostles; those who, together with the succession of the episcopate, have received the certain gift of truth."

In 398 at the 4th Council of Carthage, bishops, and that means all clergy too, were forbidden to read any books not written by Christians!

When the Church succeeded in fully taking over in Europe by circa 500 AD, instead of an age of love and light as 'Gentle Jesus' might have been expected to bring, we got the Dark Ages, centuries of ignorance, of a darkness in education (read only the Bible, burn all other texts), science (no knowledge unless it is in the Bible), history (only what is written in the Bible), medicine (likewise), art (only 'approved' art on approved religious themes, thank you). Like Soviet Communism at its worst? A thousand years later, Galileo had to recant his truth to save being butchered by a church dedicated to maintaining power and ignorance.

This was a religion based on enforced lies, deceit, fabrications and fantasies and aimed at mass brainwashing. Remarkably successful it was too, for an incredibly long time – but enough.

God, school, purgatory, guilt, flagellation:

I remember at school chapel services repeating parrot fashion the Nicaean Creed, the cornerstone of Christianity. I repeated it without knowing what it really meant. Like so many, I was a 'Christian' because I'd been told I was a Christian and everyone else was a Christian. I didn't understand the Creed but I knew it meant I was a bad person because there was no way I could live up to it or ever be good enough for this God-Chap and his One and Only Absolutely Perfect Son. I was a religious failure and therefore a personal failure and would always be so, and 'God' had nothing much good for me except pain and hellishness. The 'Public' boarding School I attended certainly made sure every day contained its portion of suffering, thus proving again and again my utter lack of worth in the eyes of both 'God' and his representatives, the human authorities.

The education system certainly took up the punishment theme of the Bible to the full, as the use of cane, birch and other torture instruments was 'normal' right up to the 1970s in Britain. The wonderful movie *If...* (1969) showed a graphic and accurate portrayal of the 'joys' of corporal punishment, public school style.

At the 'Great Public Schools' – so imitated around the Christian world and often run by religious groups – much flagellation was done by masters and more was handed over to the boy prefects who were armed with fearsome canes two to three feet long and the power to beat on the backside those they chose for the most pettifogging and contrived reasons. (Early lessons in corruption?) That means 17- to 18-year-old boys with full 'god' and schoolmaster-given permission and encouragement to attack the backsides of 13, 14, 15 and 16-year old boys who were supposed to bend over, present their rears and 'take it like a man.' Marquis de Sade, did you get your first experiences in one of these establishments? One thing is for sure, the dominatrixes of Great Britain, and much of Christianized Europe and America, have been kept busy for centuries by the ex-pupils of these 'great' establishments reliving aspects of their schooldays.

Here is the Bible-God-Chap supporting the brutalization of young boys:

"He that spareth the rod, hateth his son." — *Proverbs 13:24*

"Withhold not correction from the child: for if thou beatest him with the rod, he shall not die. Thou shalt beat him with the rod, and shalt deliver his soul from hell." Proverbs 23:13-14

I wonder how many schoolmasters through the ages have thanked 'god' regularly for such biblical injunctions to enable them to 'righteously' enjoy themselves at the expense of those unfortunates entrusted to their 'care.' Brutalized boys grow into brutal men, just the kind of morons an empire needs for its army who will obey orders without question, though the ones brutalized 'righteously' and 'for their own good' in the boarding school system tend to become men who live in deep denial of their true feelings and their true nature. And, with their memory semi-erased and their emotional life truncated, they happily send their sons to such establishments so they can be flagellated into the 'right kind of man' too. And all 'FOR THEIR OWN GOOD,' of course. (Read *The Making Of Them* by Nick Duffell. Details in Resources)

Here is Mark Twain reflecting on his boyhood.

"The mind that becomes soiled in youth can never again be washed clean. I know this by my own experience, and to this day I cherish an unappeasable bitterness against the unfaithful guardians of my young life, who not only permitted but compelled me to read an unexpurgated Bible through before I was fifteen years old. None can do that and ever draw a clean, sweet breath again this side of the grave."

When it comes to religious flagellation, the 14th century Saint Catherine of Siena, it is reported, whipped herself three times every day; once for her own sins, once for the sins of others, and once for the sins of the world. The 11th century zealot Dominicus Loricatus once repeated the entire Psalter (a collection of the psalms and other 'inspirational' material) twenty times in one week, accompanying each psalm with a hundred lash-strokes to his back. Members of Opus Dei wear a nasty buckle of spikes strapped on their thighs to keep them in constant something or other....

Well, whatever turns you on... or off! (More in Chapter 7)

Belief without knowledge:

The Nicaean Creed, far from being some great God-inspired treatise of truth, was cobbled together in AD 325 after bitter arguments and blows between factions of 318 bishops – and later revised and revised again. It is important to realize that early Christianity was composed of many small cult groups who all had their own beliefs and hierarchies. Constantine brought them together to council at Nicaea and demanded that they come to unity or suffer dire consequences. Let us now look at that incredible document now with more ancient eyes....

From the Earth-based cultures point of view, way back in the old world before male-monotheist religions and the whole concept of belief in dogmas, it made no sense whatsoever to believe in what you didn't know. If you take on a belief without actually knowing through experience, how can you ever come to actually 'know' anything? The ancients studied nature and learned through experience. If they received a 'spiritual revelation', they would test it out and see if it worked before fully accepting it.

Surely the real adventure of life is to find out about life, to explore the Universe and how it works, to come to know more of the Great Mystery that is Existence?

The Creed says one must believe in Jesus Christ as the only begotten son of God. If the rest of us humans are not begotten of God, surely there must be a far more powerful deity who has given birth to billions of humans over a vast sea of time, to say nothing of all the animals, plants, planets, suns and galaxies of the manifest Universe?

The Creed says we must believe that Jesus is made of the same substance as the Father and therefore not the same as us mere humans. Therefore he had to be born of a virgin, through a path other than the dreaded sex. That was fine until it was realized that if his mother was born through sex, the image was rather blown. His mother then also had to be born of a virgin. History doesn't record (as far as I know) whether they got to his grandmother – and great-grandmother – to make them virginally born too.

We are told to believe that Jesus, 'the only son of God' came to earth as a human and will return to sit in judgment over the rest of us. We all are supposed to live up to his impossible ideal or be judged wanting. What a great way to frighten people into self-rejection and submission. Bang goes self-worth and love and care for yourself. Jesus is reported to have said 'Love your neighbour as yourself.' Wonderful sentiment but something got lost in the yourself bit. Loving yourself has largely become equated with debauchery, sin and selfishness. I know what ribaldry and put-downs I will get in most circum-stances if I declare that I love myself. Just imagine saying that to a circle of acquaintances in the pub!

We are told that only through Jesus can we get to heaven and a reasonable afterlife. Jesus is the only doorway into a heavenly future. So at a stroke, all other paths, everybody else's spirituality, are condemned as useless, and so it then becomes a Christian's 'duty' to convert everyone else … or conquer them, kill them, eliminate their 'godless' culture, take their lands – 'in the name of God.' How convenient for an emperor-dictator-murderer such as Constantine. And later emperors, popes, the Inquisition etc. What a great foundation for a world domination cult.

Here is an extract on the subject of murder and torture from *The Christ Conspiracy* by Acharya S (p10):

"… Christian proponents had the right to purge the earth of 'evil' and to convert the 'heathen' to the 'true faith.' Over a period of more than a millennium, the Church would bring to bear in this 'purification' and 'conversion' to the religion of the 'Prince of Peace' the most horrendous torture methods ever devised, in the end slaughtering tens of millions worldwide.

"These 'conversion' methods by Catholics against men, women and children, Christians and Pagans alike, included burning, hanging and torture of all manner, using the tools described in Fourth Maccabees. Women and girls had hot pokers and sharp objects slammed up their vaginas, often after priests had raped them. Men and boys had their penises and testicles crushed or ripped or cut off. Both genders and all ages had their skin pulled off with hot pincers and their tongues ripped out, and were subjected to diabolical machinery designed for the weakest parts of the body, such as knees, ankles, elbows and fingertips, all of which were crushed. Their legs and arms were broken with sledgehammers, and, if there was anything left of them, they were hanged or burned alive. Nothing more evil could possibly be imagined, and from this absolute evil came the 'rapid' spread of Christianity.

"So far this despicable legacy and crime against humanity remains unavenged and its main culprit unpunished, not only standing intact but inexplicably receiving the undying and unthinking support of hundreds of millions.…This acquiescence is the result of the centuries of destruction and degradation of their ancestors' cultures, which demoralized them and ripped away their spirituality and heritage."

Truly horrendous.

And isn't it something that 'Gentle Jesus' who, like Buddha, supposedly advocated poverty and humility, eventually became the mythic figurehead for one of the world's pre-eminent money-making organizations. My namesake (Oh horrors!)

Pope Leo X exclaimed, "*What profit hath not that fable of Christ brought us!*" (Barbara G. Walker. 'The woman's encyclopedia'.)

The blunt fact is that 'Jesus Christ' actually had little discernable effect on history at all. Before Jesus, Rome was the dominant controller empire of the world. After the empire collapsed, it was replaced by domination and control through the Roman Church with 'Jesus' on the cross as the figure for the mind-controlling, spirit-numbing concepts of original sin and guilt. One method of power and control was simply replaced by another. And, 'My God', hasn't it been successful, just look at how many millions are still in-the-lie today!

Time to Wake Up…..

Here is an interesting current oddity. I understand Anglican clergy must *still - even today* - swear to agree to the so-called 'Thirty-nine Articles of Faith' set by Elizabeth 1st and her parliament and which all citizens had to believe or else be condemned as heretics (which virtually amounted to a death sentence). It starts with the usual all-male suspects:

"*God consists of three persons, the father, the son, and Holy Ghost.*"

Later, however, there are some really interesting edicts like these:

"*All deserve God's wrath and damnation, but there is no condemnation of believers who are baptized.*"

Woe betide any unfortunate who is not baptized, and if you don't believe what you are ordered to, you'd better keep your mouth well shut! Then we get this:

"*Predestination to life is the everlasting purpose of God, to deliver from curse and damnation those whom he has chosen in Christ, to bring them everlasting salvation.*"

100

So the God-Chap first curses everybody and then chooses some to be saved from his own curses?

Lastly here is another piece which is great for lazy people:

"Our righteousness before God comes, not by our works, but by the merit of Christ. Therefore we are justified only by faith and not by works."

Just believe what you are told and all will be OK. Never mind action, never mind soiling yourself with work, never mind actually doing things for other people; just believe the 'right beliefs' and the god-chap will look after you. Amazing!

Erroneous ideas of perfection require a 'devil':

Male-monotheism through Christianity has embraced the idea of God as 'perfect' and human beings as born in sin, bad people needing redemption. This necessitates the invention of a counter force to explain all the things that go wrong so 'God' can stay pure and unsullied, and be seen to do only the good things of creation. So they had to invent 'The Devil' to take responsibility for everything they didn't like and anything that went wrong. Perhaps I could say 'Devil-Chap' (Satan-Chap) as from the religionists' point of view, he is all-male, too.

If we go back to pre-male-monotheist cultures, we find no devil but instead representative figures of human egotism and stupidity such as 'Coyote,' the Native American trickster figure who keeps landing in the mire of his own cunning plans, and 'Mulla Nasrudin', the Indian comic figure who screws up all over the place.

But if God is already perfect, why on earth did S/He bother with all this creation, with this planet, with the galaxy, with the whole Universe? The Creator must have some reason, some purpose however mysterious, to Create Itself into The

Creation. Furthermore, how could a 'perfect' God keep screwing up so badly that this other Devil-Chap keeps getting in and making a mockery of his plans? If the God-Chap was at all perfect, or even competent, he would have sussed out the devil-chap long ago and got him sorted!

Surely the reason for God, The Source, to create It's Self into all this Life, The Universe and Everything is to gain experience, to grow, to develop, to **evolve**.

"Life is the manifested evidence of the Source's Desire for Evolution."

— The same desires that are in us, though on a giant scale. We live within God, The Source, Infinite Creator/Creation, so how can we not feel the same feelings as God and God the same feelings as us, albeit at a vastly different level of existence and of consciousness?

The metaphysical Bible puts it like this:

Satan is the 'Devil', a state of mind formed by man's personal ideas of his power and completeness and sufficiency apart from God. Besides at times puffing up the personality, this satanic thought often turns about and, after having tempted one to do evil, discourages the soul by accusing it of sin. Summed up, it is the state of mind in man that believes in its own sufficiency independent of its Creative Source.

Satan = egotism. It is interesting too, that the voice of Jehovah in the Old Testament is very like the expression of the male ego in full flood of patriarchal dominance.

The notion of perfection within earthly existence is a silly, misguided myth created by cultures that have lost their connection with the natural roots of existence. Just look at nature. The whole of nature is perfect in an overall sense but try to find a flower without a blemish, an animal without a mark of some kind, a human without a problem, a tree without a dead branch? Everything has its imperfection – that's nature. Perfection / imperfection live together in balance. Look at the lupin flower. You will never find a perfectly flowering lupin. (except a plastic one of course!) When it is fully bloomed at the bottom, some of the top is dead, and when it is flowering perfectly at the top, the bottom hasn't yet budded.

These religious ideas of rigid perfection and unchangeabililty of God and 'His' separation from 'His' creation have caused immeasurable misery, confusion and loss of personal inner authority. The absurd travesties of 'original sin', the trashing of the proper meaning and teaching of the story of Adam and Eve and the use of the Jesus story to impregnate people with guilt just for being normal have left us floundering in a sea of cockeyed back-to-front life-myths that leave us disenfranchised from our own selves and from the very Nature that gave rise to us in the first place.

Creation – nature – includes all; earthquakes happen and people get hurt, volcanoes erupt and whole towns get swept away. That's just the way it is. But good and evil are what we humans do. Creation just does its thing! In the words of Sufi poet Rumi (1207-1273):

'Out beyond ideas of
right-doing and wrong-doing
There is a field
I'll meet you there'

Chapter 7
Religion and sex.
The male-monotheist 'God-Chap'
Hates Sex, Women and Human Bodies!

How do you feel about sex? Do you enjoy it, revel in it, let you body go with its natural impulses? Give and receive pleasure freely and lovingly with your partner?

How do you feel about women? Do you consider woman equal to man, albeit different? That women are fully half the human race and worthy of the highest esteem?

How do you feel about men? Do you feel they too are equal, though not superior? That they are vulnerable, emotional beings also worthy of the highest esteem?

How do you feel about your body? Do you treat it as your temple, look after it, exercise it, care for it, love it?

Well, if you think, feel or do any of those things you are way out of order with mainstream Christian thought and teaching for around 1700 years. Take a look at what follows – and prepare to laugh – or weep – or both at the same time.....

Here are some early Church fathers speaking about sex and marriage, thanks to Barbara G Walker in *WEMS*:

Origen (Origenes Adamantius, Christian father, ca: 185-254 AD. An Egyptian who wrote in Greek, exerting a powerful influence on the early Greek church. Made a saint but declared a heretic three centuries later.): *"Matrimony is impure and unholy, a means to sexual passion."*

To St Jerome, the primary purpose of a man of God was to *"Cut down with an axe of Virginity the wood of Marriage."*

And: *"Every man who loves his wife is guilty of adultery"*!

"Whosoever looketh on a woman to lust after her hath committed adultery with her already in his heart." Jesus in Matthew 5.28-30. That includes just about every non-gay man ever!

To St Ambrose, marriage was a crime against God because it changed the state of virginity that God gave every man and woman at birth. Marriage was prostitution of the members of Christ, and *"Married people ought to blush at the state in which they are living."*

To Turtullian, marriage was a moral crime, *"more dreadful than any punishment or any death."* It was 'spurcitiae' – 'obcenity' or 'filth.'

To Tatian, marriage was corruption, *"A polluted and foul way of life."* It seems he had such an effect on Syrian churches that only celibate men could become Christians!

St. Bernard said it was easier for a man to bring the dead back to life than to live with a woman without endangering his soul.

A little bit of the history of sex, marriage and celibacy: (Note: his-story, not her-story!)

325 AD: The Council of Nicaea decreed that no priest will be allowed to marry after ordination.

385 AD: Pope Siricius decreed that priests married before ordination must not make love with their wives afterwards. (May have been some slippage in getting the Nicaean Decree out to the provinces?)

Pope Gregory 'The Great,' (590-604 AD) decreed that all sexual desire was sinful and only for producing children.

1074 AD: Pope Gregory VII decreed all priests must be celibate.

Late 20th century the truth of what 'celibate' priests really did with their sexual energy for years starts to become public knowledge.

Note that St Peter the 'Rock,' on whom the church was said to be founded, was said to be a married man.

Well, there you have it. That is the old Christian view of marriage and women and that is from the time when Christianity was new and at its prime.

The Bible-God-Chap REALLY Hates Women:

Here are just a few of the Bible's misogynistic statements:

St Paul in the first letter to Timothy decrees:

"Let the women learn in silence with all subjection."

"But I suffer a woman not to teach, nor to usurp authority over a man, but to be in silence. For Adam was first formed then Eve." That Adam and Eve crap again!

"And Adam was not deceived, but the woman being deceived was in the transgression." — I Timothy 2:14-15

And again! St Paul reasons:

"For a man did not originally spring from woman, but woman was made out of man; and was not created for woman's sake, but woman for the sake of man."

So yet again the misconstruing of the myth of Adam and Eve is used to hold woman in subjugation.

"Wives submit to your husbands for the husband is the head of the wife as Christ is head of the Church. Now if the Church submits to Christ so should wives submit to their husbands in everything."

And this:

"In like manner also, that women adorn themselves in modest apparel, with shamefacedness and sobriety; not with braided hair, or gold, or pearls, or costly array; but (which becometh women professing godliness) with good works." — I Timothy 2: 9-13

Well, what a charter of women's un-rights! And all based on a thorough misreading of the story of Adam and Eve. Remember, 'God' proved to be the liar and the Serpent the truth teller. Eve was a great deal more prescient that Adam. And without Eve's courage to challenge 'God,' none of us would be here! So Paul is wrong on all counts. The very fabric of the Christian religion depends wholly on the misinterpretation of the myth of Adam and Eve. Here is Mary Daly from *Before God the Father* (Beacon Press, Boston 1973 p.69):

"Take the snake, the fruit tree, and the woman from the tableau, and we have no fall, no frowning Judge, no inferno, no everlasting punishment – hence no need of a Savior. Thus the bottom falls out of the whole Christian theology."

By contrast it seems the early Gnostic Christians, the real ones before the literalists got control who were later branded as heretics, had a very different idea. Here is Tertullian, appalled at the role of Gnostic women:

"… women of the heretics, how wanton they are! For they are bold enough to teach, to dispute, to enact exorcisms, to undertake cures, it may be even to baptize!"

And just generally appalled:

"The judgment upon your sex endures even today; and with it inevitably endures your position at the bar of justice. (Woman) you are the gateway to hell."

—Tertullian in *De Cultu Feminarium*

What is it about saints?? Is part of being a saint that you hate woman, hate the feminine? Try this from St Jerome, Epistle 107:

*"I am aware that some have laid it down that virgins of Christ must not bathe with eunuchs or married women, because the former still have minds of men and the latter present the ugly spectacle of swollen bellies. For my part I say that **mature girls should not bathe at all, because they ought to blush to see themselves naked.**"*

Hysterical! Where was he at? What on earth have all these 'saints' suffered so they hate and disparage their mothers, women and the feminine?

St. Gregory of Nazianzum:

"Women — a foe to friendship, an inescapable punishment, a necessary evil."

"Among save beasts, none is found so harmful as woman."

According to Saturninus, God made only two kinds of people — good men and evil women!

Here is St Paul with another tenet clearly prohibits women from being ministers or otherwise speaking in church:

"Let your women keep silence in the churches: for it is not permitted unto them to speak." — I Corinthians 14:34

St Clement of Alexandria in the second century wrote:

"Every woman should be filled with shame by the thought that she is a woman."

Isn't that just something! I shall write that again bold and underlined so you don't miss it!

'EVERY WOMAN SHOULD BE FILLED WITH SHAME BY THE THOUGHT THAT SHE IS A WOMAN'

Well you can't get more explicit than that. I trust all you Catholic Ladies like this sentiment and agree with your saint. And do you realize that up to the mid 16th century (see below), you were not even credited with having souls by your church. You were truly considered, and treated, like an inferior species.

This is history, women, **HIS**-story. Are you happy with it?

What about **HER**-story, womens' story, your story?

Ah, but there is another answer, it seems. The Gospel of Thomas 114 says this:-

"Simon Peter said to them: '*Let Mary go forth from among us, for* **women are not worthy of the life.**'

Jesus said: '*Behold, I shall lead her, that I may* **make her male***, in order that she also may become a living spirit like you males. For every woman who makes herself male shall enter into the kingdom of heaven.*'"

There you are ladies – Jesus says you have to become male in order to be worthy of the Kingdom! – Incredible.

Turtullian – yes him again – endeavored to explain why women deserve their inferior status:

"*And do you not know you are an Eve? The sentence of God on this sex of yours lives in this age: the guilt must necessarily live too.*"

They all love to dump guilt on women, don't they. He continues:

"You are the devil's gateway: you are the unsealer of that tree: you are the first deserter of the divine law: you are she who persuaded him whom the devil was not valiant enough to attack. You destroyed so easily God's image, man. On account of your desert – that is death – even the son of god had to die."

So women get blamed for the death of Jesus! Hysterical! But Tertullian was mild compared to what was to come later. Boethius, a 6th century Christian wrote in *The Consolation of Philosophy*:

"Woman is a temple built upon a sewer."

And in Job 25:4 we read: *"How then can man be justified with God? Or how can he be clean that is born of woman?"*

Remember – Christians are supposed to believe that all this is the literal 'Word of God'

These guys must have had terrible problems with women's genitals and with sex and birthing. At the **Council of Macon** in AD585, it has been said that the bishops voted as to whether woman had souls at all – and decided not. That means they voted that their mothers were soulless! (There is some doubt as to the veracity of this story, however.)

Centuries later at the **Council of Trent** which took place from 1545 to 1563 in Trento, Northern Italy, I'm told it took one day for them to decide that animals don't have souls and 21 days and a close vote (majority of 3, I read) to decide that , after all, women do! Amazing!

It seems there was no proper Christian marriage for centuries right up to and beyond the Council of Trent. This Council decreed that a person who even hinted that the state of matrimony might be more blessed than celibacy would be declared *anathema*. That means accursed and excommunicated!

This madness is our history and that bit is only 450 years ago. Here is the worst of all, from the infamous and appalling *Malleus Maleficorum* or *Witch's Hammer*:

"Because the female sex is more concerned with things of the flesh than men; because being formed from a man's rib, they are only imperfect animal and crooked whereas man belongs to a privileged sex from whose midst Christ emerged." Yet again it comes back to the mis-interpretation of Adam and Eve. (See Chapter 8 for more on the Inquisition.)

Woman-beating was a normal Christian man's duty. The *Decretum* of 1140 said: *"It is right that he whom woman led into wrongdoing should have her under his direction so that he may not fail a second time through female levity."*

Friar Cherubino's 15th century rules of marriage made the husband the wife's sole judge: *"Scold her sharply, bully and terrify her. And if this doesn't work take up a stick and beat her soundly, for it is better to punish the body and correct the soul than to damage the soul and spare the body... Then readily beat her, not in rage but out of charity and concern for her soul, so that the beating will redound to your merit."* — Abbreviated from Barbara G Walker, *WEMS*

Bishop Epiphanus in the 4th century wrote: *(Also quoted from p26 of above)*

"God came down from heaven, the Word clothed himself in flesh from a holy virgin, not, assuredly, that the virgin should be adored, nor to make a goddess of her, nor that we should offer sacrifice in her name, nor that, now after so many generations, women should once again be appointed priests....(God) gave her no charge to minister baptism or bless disciples, nor did he bid her rule over the earth."

He was having a bit of difficulty making sure he got in all the things that shouldn't be done, wasn't he!

In the 5th century, the Catholic Church got really powerful. By 435 they had a law that threatened any heretic in the Roman Empire with death, and the only other legal religion was Judaism. However, Jews were isolated and intermarriage carried the same penalty as adultery. Guess what that was – in this patriarchal society it was death for the woman, of course! What about the man? Not recorded.

Here are some anti-woman quotations from the Old Testament. Numbers 25 is interesting in its sheer violence: "... *Then the people started to have immoral relations with the daughters of Moab. And the women came calling the people to the sacrifices of their Gods... So Israel attached itself to Ba'al of Pe'or and the anger of Jehovah began to blaze against Israel. Hence Jehovah said to Moses, 'Take all the head ones of the people and expose them to Jehovah toward the sun that the burning anger of Jehovah may turn back from Israel. Each one of you KILL his men who have an attachment with the Ba'al of Pe'or'.*

But look, a man of the sons of Israel came bringing near to his brothers a Mid'ian-ite woman before Moses eyes... and the priest caught sight of it, he at once took a lance in his hand. Then he went after the man... and pierced both of them through, the man of Israel and the woman through her genital parts....And those who died from the scourge amounted to **twenty-four thousand."**

Jehovah-God did an extraordinary lot of killing.

Here is an odd one from Deuteronomy 25:11: "*In case men struggle together with one another and the wife of one has come near to deliver her husband out of the hand of the one striking him, and she has thrust out her hand and grabbed hold of him by his privates, you must then amputate her hand. Your eye must feel no sorrow."*

What?? A wife tries to help her husband and has her hand cut off! Reading the Old Testament makes it so clear what an incredibly male-dominated, warlike, combative and violent time it was. And 'God' was the most warlike and violent of all. A very important question is - which comes first, 'God' or human society. Or perhaps better put - does 'God' create humans or do humans create 'God'? Clearly most of the time, it is we humans who create 'God' to suit our prevailing needs and fit our beliefs to suit. So in a violent, warlike time when the greatest need is to be ready for combat – and the Middle East and Europe at the time had been in constant war for centuries with empires coming and going and constant threats from neighbors – then a god of war was required to keep the people in battle mode and the males in dominance. So that is what we got. But let us stop pretending this has anything whatsoever to do with the real God-Creator-Creation.

The Bible is the words of men and the 'gods' that the rulers required to bind their people together. By encouraging men to be warlike and dominant, to subdue not just anyone who doesn't agree with their dogma but the animals and plants and everything else around as well, the Bible has given carte blanche to the worst aspects of human nature and a 'god' who epitomizes them. So what about love? No person can make love and war at the same time. By frustrating the natural sexual instinct and making it wrong, and telling people God will be sending them to hell unless they crush their own natural instincts, the Bible version of religion has condemned us to an appalling travesty of the life we could have.

The Reformation:

In the 15th and 16th centuries, the Reformation spurned a load of virulent anti-woman preachers. Here is Martin Luther:

"Girls begin to talk and to stand on their feet sooner than boys because weeds always grow more quickly than good crops."

What an incredibly convenient rationalization! Apparently the Lutherans debated whether women were really human beings at all! Martin Luther again, from *Table Talk:*

"Women … have but small and narrow chests, and broad hips, to the end that they should remain at home, keep house, and bear and bring up children."

Sounds like a line from a Monty Python sketch. It would be funny except that it's real and countless women have suffered for such upside-down be-<u>lie</u>-fs.

John Knox, the Scottish Presbyterian leader also had little truck with women. From *The First Blast of the Trumpet Against the Monstrous Regiment of Women*, published 1558:

"Nature doeth paint them to be weak, frail, impatient, feeble and foolish; and experience hath declared them to be unconstant, variable, cruel, and lacking in the spirit of counsel."

And this: *"To promote a woman to bear rule, superiority, dominion or empire, above any realm, nation, or city; contumely to God, a thing most contrarious to his revealed will and approved ordinance, and finally it is the subversion of good order, of all equity and justice."*

Well, I guess Queen Elizabeth 1 was not a Presbyterian. Nor Queen Elizabeth 2, or Margaret Thatcher or all those women MPs and woman leaders of one kind and another. I wonder if there are still any Presbyterians now – and are they all men? And how do they multiply and create more little Presbyterians?

And now – Anti-human preaching extraordinaire:

Jonathan Edwards, a Calvinist New England theologian in the mid-1700s:

"(You are) a little, wretched, despicable creature: a worm, a mere nothing, and less than nothing; a vile insect that has risen up in contempt against the majesty of heaven and earth."

Many years ago I was researching in a library for something (ir)religious I could do in a comedy routine and to my delight I came across Edwards. The book said he was a 'major religious thinker of his day', which made me cackle with delighted amazement at sheer human imbecility. Major religious thinker, indeed! That is an insult to the noble art of thinking. So let us look at some more of this 'major religious thinker's' astonishing 'religious thoughts' and enjoy a few good laughs. I suggest you think *Monty Python*, especially John Cleese in his Hitler / Basil Fawlty mode, all virulence and funny postures. Feel hate for everybody, screw up your face into a paroxysm of barely controlled violence, feel your body almost paralytic with stress, and then read this (verbatim from an Edwards sermon) to your friends, spitting venom:

"The God that holds you over the pit of hell, much as one holds a spider or some loathsome insect over the fire, abhors you and is dreadfully provoked, his wrath towards you burns like fire; he looks upon you as worthy of nothing else but to be cast into the fire; he is of purer eyes than to bear to have you in his sight, you are ten thousand times so abominable in his eyes as the most hateful and venomous serpent is in ours."

Wow! You couldn't make it up. What was wrong with this guy? If he hated people so much, he must have deplored himself. Try this next one for the sheer appalling quality of fear and threat he is putting out:

"The bow of god's wrath is bent, and the arrow made ready on the string, and justice bends the arrow at your heart, and strains the

bow, and it is nothing but the mere pleasure of God, and that of an angry God, without the promise or obligation at all, that keeps the arrow one moment from being made drunk with your blood."

Fabulous! Well fabulous to make comedy out of but not so good for the poor wretches who were in his congregation and had to listen to this soul-destroying sh*t Sunday after Sunday. Much worse for the unfortunates who actually took it to heart and believed it.

But there is more. Look at this next piece with sexual awareness. What sort of love and passion do you think this preacher might have enjoyed in his life? What sort of passion would lead a man to preach in this way? I know what I think but see what it says to you:

"The wrath of God is like the **great waters that are damned** for the present. **They increase more and more,** and **rise higher and higher,** till an **outlet is given:** and the **longer the stream is stopped, the more rapid and mighty** is its course, when once it is **let loose.** It is true, that judgment against your evil work has not been executed hitherto; **the floods** of God's vengeance have been withheld, but your guilt in the meantime is **constantly increasing** and you are **every day treasuring up more** wrath; the **waters are continually rising and waxing more and more mighty** and there is nothing but the mere pleasure of God that holds the waters back that are **unwilling to be stopped and press hard** to go forward.

If God should only **withdraw his hand** from the floodgate, it would **immediately fly open** and the **fiery floods of the fierceness and wrath** of God would **rush forth with inconceivable fury, and would come upon you with omnipotent power.....**

OK, I cheated! I highlighted the best bits. This guy is monstrously frustrated. He is a sexual bomb desperate to go off, and he is obviously getting no release in the normal way, so his love implodes and becomes bottled venom and hate and he seeks to control and dominate others so their love turns toxic, too. To see other people in a state of loving tenderness must have been quite unbearable to him.

Lastly, just to rub the point in, so to speak, here is one more piece of his virulence:

*"There are the black clouds of God's wrath now hanging directly over your heads, **full of the dreadful storm and big with thunder,** and were it not for the **restraining hand** of God, it would **burst forth** upon you. The sovereign pleasure of God, for the present, stays his rough wind; otherwise it would **come with fury** and your destruction would **come like a whirlwind** and you would be like the chaff on the summer threshing floor."*

— Jonathan Edwards, quoted from *Sinners in the Hands of an Angry God* (Boston, 1742)

Big ... full of ... restraining hand ... come with fury ... come like a whirlwind ...

You can almost feel him orgasming in the preachers pulpit! And this man is a 'major religious thinker'?

Well, I say *"God Save Us from religion and its thinkers."*

In the words of Stephen Fry at the Intelligence Squared debate on whether the Roman Catholic Church is a beneficial organisation, London 2010:

'...*This church is obsessed with sex, absolutely obsessed....* (Comparing with food) *The only people obsessed with food are the anorexics and the morbidly obese — and that, in erotic terms, is the Catholic Church in a nutshell*'!

Thank you, Stephen. Nail on head. Wonderful!

'God' hates the human body:

Isn't it a funny sort of 'god' who would hate his own creation. Here is St Paul:

Romans 8:5: *"For those who are in accord with the flesh set their minds on the things of the flesh, but those in accord with the spirit, on the things of the spirit."*

So far so good.

8-6: *"For the minding of the flesh means death."*

Funny, I always thought – in fact, I know – that minding the flesh, looking after the body, caring for it like it is my friend, keeps me fit, healthy and alive. *"... but the minding of the spirit means life and peace."* Yes, absolutely, but not if your body is falling apart through lack of care. Why is he so divided?

8-7: *"Because the minding of the flesh means enmity with God, for it is not under the subjection to the law of God, nor in fact can it be."*

No it doesn't! Caring for your body is caring for your human temple, given by God-Creation for the purpose of this life. No body, no life! If 'God' is against the body, he is against life itself, and he is supposed to be the Creator of all life! Well, if so – and this is the Bible so it 'must' be the 'Word-of-God' – then 'God', by his own words, is seriously psychotic as one part of him is acting against the other!

8-9: *"However, you are in harmony not with the flesh but with the spirit, if God's spirit truly dwells within you."*

Why can we not be in harmony with the flesh *and* the spirit? Seems much more whole and sensible to me.

8-13: *"For if you live in accord with the flesh you are sure to die, but if you put the practices of the body to death by the spirit, you will live."*

This verse really shows the problem. They all seem to want to attack the body as if it is the enemy. *If you kill the body, you will live?* – not in this realm you won't. Life after death – yes – but that comes naturally in due time.

Turning to James 1:15, we read: *"Thus when lust hath conceived, it bringeth forth sin, when it is finished, bringeth forth death."*

Lust, you nincompoop, brings forth new life. No lust, no babies. Try and make love without it! Jolly difficult and requires a whole lot of fantasy - and that's a jolly big sin, remember. (See Chapter 3 if you forgot already!)

Here is an Augustinian priest and chaplain to the King of Poland (From *Delumeau* in *Sin and Fear*, quoted in *The Dark Side of Christian History*, p.160): *"Follow our Lord's example, and hate your body; if you love it, strive to lose it, says holy scripture, in order to save it; if you wish to make peace with it, always go armed,* **always wage war against it; treat it like a slave,** *or soon you yourself will be its unhappy slave."*

What a miserable outlook! I have written in earlier chapters of 'saints' who seem to have been unable to keep their pants on and blamed the women for their problems. It seems that as they were unable to control their own desires, they tried everything to control, restrict and limit the natural way of the body, thinking this was somehow 'godly'.

They also lacked any sort of respect for the Earth. The Roman Empire built aqueducts, roads, houses with plumbing, washing facilities – we have all heard of Roman baths and there are relics in England – but once the Christians got to power, all that was neglected, and hygiene and 'things of the body' became considered contemptible and ungodly. In fact, it is really only in the last fifty to perhaps hundred years that decent bodily hygiene has come fully back into fashion in some Christian countries. Thanks to the leisure clubs, gyms, saunas, steam rooms and the ancient sweat lodge ceremony of the Native American people.

Personally, I treat my body as my temple, I feed it with love and care, endeavor to listen to it and respond to its needs, and I go regularly to the gym for healthy exercise and bathing. And I do my best to make loving, healthy, beautiful love when the feeling, the moment and the circumstances are right!

'God' is even against bodyparts: (No prize for guessing which ones!)

Here's Jesus as quoted in Luke 20:34-36:

"The children of this system of things marry and are given in marriage, but those who have been counted worthy of gaining that system of things and the resurrection from the dead neither marry nor are given in marriage. In fact neither can they die anymore for they are like the angels, and they are God's children by being children of the resurrection."

So to not marry, and by implication, to have no sex life, is taught as superior. Thus the anti-sexual teaching that sets people at war with themselves is authenticated and combined with a nice bit of convenient fantasy. Well, of course, if they are like angels, they will have no such problems because they will have no bodies. Angels do not have bodies!

And in Matthew 19:12, Jesus goes even further:

"For there are some eunuchs, which were so born from their mother's womb: and there are some eunuchs, which were made eunuchs of men: and there be eunuchs, which have made themselves eunuchs for the kingdom of heaven's sake. He that is able to receive it, let him receive it."

So chopping off your genitals is the most holy thing you can do!

"Origen was highly praised for having castrated himself. Justin's 'Apologia' said proudly that Roman surgeons were besieged by faithful Christian men requesting the operation. Tertullian declared: 'The Kingdom of Heaven is thrown open to eunuchs.' Justin advised that Christian boys be emasculated before puberty, so their virtue was permanently protected.

Men - just imagine having that forced on you before you knew what it meant. Women in some parts of the world have had just that – genital mutilation – for centuries and it still goes on. (More in Chapter 10)

There are numerous sayings of Paul which suggest that he himself was castrated and that he rated it as necessary for the highest spiritual achievement:

"I bear in my body the marks of the Lord Jesus." — Galations 6.17)

"Moreover, those who belong to Christ Jesus impaled the flesh together with its passions and lusts." — Galations 5:24

"I would they were even cut off which trouble you." — Galations 5:12

(Note: the words 'cut off' are a euphemism for castrated)

From Barbara G. Walker, *The Woman's Encyclopedia of Myths and Secrets*, Harper, San Francisco. pp. 146 / 776).

So there you are. Now you know what to do, Christian fellows, if you really want to prove yourselves really good Christian Men.

Seriously though, this really takes the lid off Christian sexuality. No wonder I had such a terrible, confused puberty while trying to be a good Christian. I still had my sinful member daily or even by the minute, trying to lead me away from 'God' and into sin, sin and every day more sin!

Remember that saying: A man thinks of sex every six minutes? Oh sorry, not minutes, seconds! No wonder Christianity has nothing to offer people at puberty other than don't, mustn't and shouldn't. No wonder there are no puberty rites and no guidance for adolescents going through this crucial period in their lives. It is a religion that, albeit subtly and perhaps unconsciously, is recommending castration as the most godly state of being!

(I must say though, after recent revelations, that if celibate priests became castrated priests instead, it might save an awful lot of trouble for the church!)

The body as the enemy; sex as a great evil; woman as an inferior being without a soul; castrated men the most holy? What was wrong with these people? Hadn't they noticed that without sex, none of us gets to be here. None, not one, no one gets to be born. And furthermore, you need a woman for it, men simply cannot do it on their own, however hard they try.

Now let us look for a moment at how later followers of this body-hating belief system made out. Here is Ignatius Loyola, founder of the Jesuits:

"I am mere dung, I must ask our Lord that when I am dead my body be thrown on the dungheap to be devoured by the birds and dogs.... Must this not be my wish in punishment for my sins?"

— Delumeau - Catholicism between Luther and Voltaire

And from John Calvin:

"We are all made of mud, and this mud is not just on the hem of our gown, or on the sole of our boots or in our shoes. We are full of it, we are nothing but mud and filth both inside and outside."

— Delumeau – Sin and fear

(Both thanks to Helen Ellerbe, *The Dark Side of Christian History*.)

We can go back to Genesis 3:17-19 for the origin of these sentiments: *"Cursed is the ground on your account. In pain you will eat its produce all the days of your life. And thorns and thistles it will grow for you, and you must eat the vegetation of the field. In the sweat of your face you will eat bread until you return to the ground, for out of it you were taken. For dust you are and to dust you will return."*

I have criticized Saul-Paul quite a bit in this chapter so here is something he got right:

"But if there be no resurrection of the dead, then is Christ not risen: And if Christ be not risen, then our preaching is in vain, and your faith is also vain. Yea, and we are found false witnesses of God, because we have testified of God that he raised up Christ whom he raised not up, if so be that the dead rise not.

— Corinthians 15:13-16

YES, YES, YES, YES, YES, YES, YES AND YES AGAIN!

And here is Freidrich Neitzsche's opinion:-

Saul killed the Christianity of Jesus and replaced it with a counterfeit version of the gospel, a vision of hatred produced in the fetid confines of a Pharisaic mind'

This Bible-God-Chap punishes, curses, hates, kills at random and demands our absolute loyalty - or else…. He is nothing remotely like a God of Love.

Yet his believers keep telling us he is a loving god??

What went so wrong?

But that is not all of it. Prepare for something even worse...........

Chapter 8
Religion and violence:
The Inquisition – 600 years+ holocaust.

We are accustomed to thinking of the terrible wipeout of the Jews in the WWII as The Holocaust but there is a much greater holocaust in our history and it still affects deeply the collective psyche of the descendents of Europeans. I refer to the centuries of burnings of so-called witches and heretics. It seems even Sir Thomas More, a man for perhaps not as many seasons as advertised, was not averse to burning heretics – and that even included people caught reading the Bible in English. This, at its simplest, means he was happy to torture and murder those who didn't agree with him.

From the time of the imposition of the Nicaean Creed by Constantine, so-called heresy – i.e. anyone who didn't agree with the orthodoxy of the day – was persecuted vehemently in order to keep the faith 'pure'. In other words, everyone had to agree to 'believe' what those in authority decreed was 'the truth' or else suffer persecution, torture and death. Super mega mind-control!

Once Stalin got hold of Russia he systematically imposed his will upon the politics, politicians and people of the day by murdering or banishing to Siberia any who wouldn't submit to him, thus imposing a tyranny of belief in (his version of) communism. Similarly the Roman Church imposed its will upon the politics and people of its day and forced upon them a whole set of beliefs with the threat of torture and death.

George Orwell came up with the wonderful concept of the 'thought police' in his novel *1984*. But it was not in any way a new idea. They were around for hundreds of years as an arm of the Roman Catholic Church.

It seems that, prior to Constantine, maybe as few as 2,000 people were tortured and murdered in the process of the battle by Rome against the early Christians up to the imposition of Christianity as the official religion of the empire. However, in the centuries following, as many as 25 million were murdered by the church as heretics. Add in the 12 million murdered in the conquest of the Americas plus the witch burnings and all that went on over approximately 14 centuries in order to impose this tyranny, and some say the total could well be in excess of 100 million. That is a lot of murder. Especially when done in the service of something people call 'god.'

It is important to realize that the length of time and the scope of this holocaust completely dwarfs those of either Hitler or Stalin. It went on in different parts of Europe from the 300s to as recently as about 1800s with the 'witches' of Salem in the US. It is estimated that between 9 and 12 million people, mainly women, were burned across the face of Europe as witches from the 12th century to the 17th century by the Unholy Inquisition.

Why am I going on about this? Because it is like a folk memory, deep in the psyche, a deep sense of fear and dread, a deep sense of disconnection from the Real Divine because so many terrible things were done in the name of God and Christ, so many centuries of living under the threat of torture and death if you didn't 'believe' and profess and act as you were ordered. Just as Russia is recovering from about sixty years of Stalinist totalitarianism, so Europe is still recovering from more than a thousand years of Roman Catholic totalitarianism.

To dare to find true spirituality and connection to the Real Source, we must divorce ourselves from these religious imposters, and that means to confront centuries of fear and terror that have been embedded in the psyche of our ancestors and handed down to us subliminally. Once we truly reframe ourselves as part of The Whole, The Divine, The Creation, The All-That-Is, The Great Spirit, God (the real God that is *ALL-THAT-IS* and *ALL-MIGHTY*), we are no longer alone but part of All-One, and the whole separatist, reductionist, belief-without-knowledge Christian, Islamic, Jewish (and other) masculinist-monotheist church edifices crumble to dust and we are set free.

To the Native American people, Holocaust means four to five hundred years of European conquest, murder, genocide, loss of homelands, loss of livelihood, loss of citizenship in their own country, prohibition of their spiritual ways, loss of their whole way of life.

Literalist Christian religion was very helpful in that it placed these people as 'lost souls' in need of 'saving.' Therefore 'god' would approve all the murder and genocide, and consider that every soul 'brought to Jesus' was worth all the bloodshed, lies and deceit.

Hell of a 'god'. And it's still going on now.

Holocaust to the Incas meant the arrival of Pizarro and his band of Spanish thugs. To the Aztecs, it meant the arrival of Cortez and his murderous army.

The Unholy Inquisition:

In some parts of what the Roman Catholic Church considered to be its empire or fiefdom, it seems that around the later 1200s, they felt they were losing control. Pope Gregory 9th appointed the Dominicans as inquisitors and ordered them to eradicate heresy everywhere. It is interesting to note that one root of the word 'heresy' is Hera, the wife of Zeus. Zeus was the Greek god of war - a role model for Jehovah – but his wife, Hera, had followers too who had different ideas, feminine ideas. And they were known as Heretics!

In and around 1308 AD in Southern France, the Cathars had different ideas, too, about God and worship, and it seems the Catholic Church was seriously frightened it was *losing control*. And losing control is not what the church-corporation was about, so something had to be done. And it was. The Dominicans moved in and, after much inquisiting, torture, prison and burning at the stake and mass slaughter, the Cathars were completely wiped out. Here is some background info:

Cathars and Catharism in the Languedoc (from http://www.languedoc-france.info):

"The Cathars were a religious group who appeared in Europe in the eleventh century, their origins something of a mystery. Records from the Roman Church mention them under various names and in various places, occasionally throwing light on basic beliefs. The Roman Church debated with itself whether they were Christian heretics or whether they were not Christians at all. In the Languedoc, famous at the time for its high culture, tolerance and liberalism, Catharism took root and gained more and more adherents during the twelfth century. By the early thirteenth century, it was probably the majority religion in the area supported by the nobility as well as the common people. This was too much for the Roman Church, some of whose own priests had become Cathars. Worst of all, Cathars of the Languedoc refused to pay their tithes.

"The Pope, Innocent (Guilty) III, called a formal crusade, appointing a series of leaders to head his (un)holy army. There followed over forty years of war against the indigenous population. In 1233 the next pope, Gregory IX, charged the Dominican Inquisition with the final solution: the absolute extirpation of the Cathars. Soon

the Franciscans would join in, too, but it is St. Dominic and his followers who have left the legacy of hatred that endures into the third millennium. During this period, some 500,000 Languedoc men women and children were massacred; the Counts of Toulouse and their vassels were dispossessed and humiliated, and their lands annexed to France. Educated and tolerant Languedoc rulers were replaced by relative barbarians; the Dominican Order was founded and the Inquisition was established to wipe out the last vestiges of resistance; persecutions of Languedoc Jews and other minorities were initiated; the high culture of the Troubadours was lost; lay learning was discouraged; tithes were enforced; the Languedoc started its economic decline, and the language of the area, Occitan, started its descent from one of the foremost languages in Europe to a regional dialect.

"At the end of the extirpation of the Cathars, the Church had convincing proof that a sustained campaign of genocide can work. It also had the precedent of an internal Crusade within Christendom, and the machinery of the first modern police state. This crusade was one of the greatest disasters ever to befall Europe. Catharism is often said to have been completely eradicated by the end of the fourteenth century. Yet there are more than a few vestiges even today, apart from the enduring memory of their martyrdom and the ruins of the famous Cathar castles. There are even Cathars alive today, or at least people claiming to be modern Cathars."

It became recognized that joining the Inquisition could be a good career move for a priest and for a certain Father Jacques Fournier, that certainly turned out to be true. He was the primary inquisitor in the Cathar village of Montaillou and after 'successfully' trying 98 cases of 'heresy,' (ie. Torturing and murdering 98 people) he became a cardinal and eventually Pope Benedict 12th. His approach to those who didn't see it his way was 'convert or die.' This demand was backed up by monstrous instruments of torture and the ultimate of burning at the stake. The people who were mostly accused of witchcraft were the healers who were mainly women and who used herbs and folk remedies of their time. These were all deemed satanic and a reason for accusation of all sorts of things.

"The Inquisition worked by ignoring all rules of natural justice. Guilt was assumed from the start. The accused had no right to see the evidence against them, or their accusers. They were not even told what the charges were against them. They had no right to legal counsel, and if exceptionally they were allowed a legal representative then the representative risked being arrested for heresy as well.

"People were charged on the say-so of hostile neighbors, known enemies and professional informers who were **paid on commission!** False accusations, if exposed, were excused if they were the result of 'zeal for the Faith.' Guilty verdicts were assured, especially since, in addition to their punishment, half of a guilty person's property was seized by the Church. (The Dominicans soon hit on the idea of digging up and trying dead people, so that they could retrospectively seize their property).

"Techniques of obtaining confessions included threats of procedures against other family members, promises of leniency in exchange for a confession, trick questions, sleep deprivation, indefinite imprisonment in a cold dark cell on a diet of bread and water, and of course a wide range of even more ghastly techniques. Torture was a favorite method of extracting confessions for offences both real and fabricated. Its use was explicitly sanctioned by Pope Guilty IV in 1252 in his bull ad extirpanda. Inquisitors and their assistants were permitted to absolve one another for applying torture. Instruments of torture, like crusaders' weapons, were routinely blessed with holy water.

"Torture was applied liberally to obtain whatever confessions were required, and sometimes just to punish people that the Church authorities did not like. Together, these techniques were responsible *for the first police state in Europe, where the only thoughts and actions permitted were those approved of by the Roman Church, where no one could be trusted, and where duty to the totalitarian authority took precedence over all other duties, whether those duties were to one's chosen sovereign, family, friends, conscience, or even to the truth."*

The atmosphere that the Inquisition produced is similar to that achieved by Stalin in his heyday, so well portrayed by George Orwell in *1984*, and also Hitler in the 1930s as he built up Nazism and the Hitler youth. In all these cases, such fear was produced that all trust broke down. Neighbors were incriminating neighbors, members of the same family were incriminating each other, and even children were denouncing their own parents. What an incredible decimation of a society. Such appalling wickedness - especially when it is in the name of 'God.'

The Inquisition went on to Spain – Iberia as it was then called. Up to this time, Christians, Moslems and Jews had lived side-by-side in a state of mutual tolerance and respect known as 'Convivensia.' This was too much for the Catholic Church and Pope Sixtus 4th sent the Inquisition to decimate that society and create years of tumult and horror. There was a pogrom against the Jews and again the demand to convert or die.

Next on the list was Venice, which at that time was a Republic in its own right and which did not wish to be dominated by Rome. This was the time when Martin Luther and the Protestants were gaining power in northern Europe and the Catholic Church was again terrified of *losing control!* A certain Bishop Caraffa was dispatched, along with the usual small army of church mercenaries, to stamp out heresy. Apparently he was very upset by the University of Padua, which was full of free-thinkers so he set out to change that. He was a true zealot and reputedly said, "Even if my own father were a heretic, I would gather the wood to burn him."

When he became Pope Paul 4th – yes for him, too, it was a good career move – he set about stamping out the Jews. He issued a Papal Bull that overturned hundreds of years of tolerance and, by 1557, Jews were forbidden to own any books except the Bible. So 200 years after being driven out of Spain, and welcomed into multi-cultural Venice, the Jews found themselves being driven out again.

Mind you, all was not milk and honey for Pope Paul 4th. It seems that when he died in 1559, Rome celebrated his death with considerable joy and partying as he was a truly hated man. Among the many acts he did to prevent human advancement, was to create a long list of books that he deemed prohibited. *And this list of forbidden books was not abolished by the Catholic Church until 1966!*

In the late 1700s, Napoleon was an important enemy of the Inquisition and worked tirelessly to keep them out of his territory. When he was deposed. they got back in to create more havoc and misery. In 1796. Spain was again terrorized by them. In 1858, they were in full swing in the papal states of Italy ... and continued for four more decades. They created untold misery for almost 600 years across the face of Europe, just to keep the power of the Catholic Church over the people.

All of us who know anything about spiritual truth know that witchcraft, as represented by them, is a totally false idea. The people they deemed witches were, in the main, healers, folk doctors, herbalists and naturopaths. Perhaps one day the real meaning of witch – 'wise woman' – will be restored to popular culture.

Here is a little about the doings of the Inquisition in England from Barbara G. Walker in *WEMS*:

"From ruthlessly organized persecutions on the continent, witch-hunts in England became largely cases of village feuds and petty spite. If crops failed, horses ran away, cattle sickened, wagons broke, women miscarried, or butter wouldn't come in the churn, a witch was always found to blame. Marion Cumlaquay of Orkney was burned in 1643 for turning herself three times widdershins to make her neighbor's barley crop rot. A tailor's wife was executed for quarrelling with her neighbor, who afterward saw a snake on his property and his children fell sick. One witch was condemned for arguing with a drunkard in an alehouse. After drinking himself into paroxysms of vomiting, he accused her of bewitching him, and he was believed.

"A woman was convicted of witchcraft for having caused a neighbor's lameness ... by pulling off her stockings. Another was executed for having admired a neighbor's baby which afterward fell out of its cradle and died. Two Glasgow witches were hanged for treating a sick child, even though the treatment succeeded and the child was cured. Joan Cason of Kent went to the gallows in 1586 for having dry thatch on her roof."

Utter madness, a whole culture gone psychotic. It must have been a truly appalling time to live. The church put back medical knowledge by an incalculable amount and brought untold misery, sickness and hardship by murdering the medical profession of the time. Imagine the Church of England branding the National Health Service as evil and killing off all the doctors and nurses by public burning! It is not out of order to suggest that the Roman Catholic Church has hindered human progress to the tune of 1000 years.

Mind you, right now another fundamentalist power is try-ing to take away our freedom to treat ourselves with vitamins and herbs. It is the 'Church of Big Pharma.' Big powerful phar-maceutical corporations are vying for legislation to prevent us buying health supplements and keeping ourselves well. It seems they'd benefit so much more if we all had to be on medication. I read an incredible statistic recently – the average American takes one medication a day and no less than 17% are on 3 medications per day. Cynically, I rather wonder if the drug company directors use their own products?

It seems probable that the Inquisition was directly respon-sible for between nine and twelve million people who were tortured, burned, and/or imprisoned in appalling circumstances. God knows how many had their lives ruined and how many cultures suffered appalling decimation. A friend researched for me and found records dating back to 1234 when 8,000 'Stedingers' (not sure who they were) were burned. Then 1239, 180 were burned for witchcraft at Montwinmer in France, and in 1275, Angela de la Barthe was burned at Toulouse.

The last in Europe would seem to be 100 people in Haeck, Germany between 1772 and 1779, 2 in Poland in 1793, several in South America in the 1800's, 1 in Illinois in 1870 and 5 in Mexico in 1877. In the last century, apparently one person was shot by a policeman in Uttenheim, Germany in 1925 on suspi-cion of being a werewolf, and one killed for 'sorcery' in France as recently as 1977! In Africa, hundreds are still killed on sus-picion of witchcraft and who knows just how much of this still goes on.

In response to church inquisitors demanding he recant his knowledge that the Earth revolves around the Sun, under threat of good Christian torture and death, Galileo Galilei said: *"I do not feel obliged to believe that the same God who has endowed us with sense, reason, and intellect has intended us to forgo their use."*

The Inquisition is a terrible blot on our history. Hitler and Stalin, appalling as they were, were short term blips by comparison, though at least they didn't pretend to be doing it for 'god.' Let us try to see nothing like it ever happens again.

"The great unmentionable evil at the centre of our culture is monotheism. From a barbaric Bronze Age text known as the Old Testament, three anti-human religions have evolved – Judaism, Christianity and Islam. These are sky-god religions. They are, literally, patriarchal – God is the Omnipotent Father – hence the loathing of women for 2000 years in those countries afflicted by the sky-god and his earthly male delegates." Gore Vidal – quoted by Richard Dawkins in 'The God Delusion'.

Chapter 9

Spirituality –

the integrated holistic God-Within-All

versus
Religion –

the male-monotheist separate God-Chap

Essential differences between spirituality and religion:

RELIGION	SPIRITUALITY
Belief in One God	Trust In Existence
God Is Separate	God Is Everything Everywhere
Set Of Specific Beliefs	Set of Tools to Discover Knowledge
God is good, Devil is evil	Good and evil are two aspects of Creation
Male priests elected by hierarchy	Spiritual teachers / shamans -male/ female, accepted through ability
Earth seen as a planet to be exploited	Earth is a living being and our Mother / nurturer
Repetitive dogma & beliefs	Structure constantly tested by what works
Masculine principle dominant	Feminine and masculine principles in balance

How does your 'God' affect medicine, science and farming?

The mental attitude of separation and feelings of need to compete or fight against other is promulgated directly by belief in this separate male God-Chap. It is reflected in both current medicine, science and even in farming. Current medical practice is mainly about fighting the enemy of germs, cancers and so on with weapons of destruction. Chemotherapy and antibiotics both work but undermine the natural systems of the patient. In extremis, the 'treatment is successful' but the patient dies.

Pre-quantum science sees a world of separate 'objects' that can be manipulated to create other useful separate objects without concern for any long term effect they may have on the environment. Current farming practice sees animals as soul-less objects which can be manipulated to produce more, who can be imprisoned in production units in ways that are quite unnatural, fed hormones and antibiotics to produce unnatural growth rates, and sometimes fed unnatural foods such as the animal products fed so ignorantly to (vegetarian) cows that caused Mad Cow Disease.

The genetic modification of crops is a modern experiment which could have dubious consequences in future years especially when you consider the invention of 'terminator' seeds which only grow once. Great for the profitability of the manufacturing corporation but quite awful for farmers and thoroughly dangerous if the idea catches on in the plant kingdom. This kind of profit before concern can only be done by a people who have lost their connection to nature and the earth and who see everything as soulless and profit as life's purpose. I am told there has been dire consequences in parts of India resulting in thousands of farmers committing suicide as their crops fail and they cannot afford replacement seeds. Here is ecologist Vandana Shiva

"Globalized industrialized food is not cheap: it is too costly for the Earth, for the farmers, for our health. The Earth can no longer carry the burden of groundwater mining, pesticide pollution, disappearance of species and destabilization of the climate. Farmers can no longer carry the burden of debt, which is inevitable in industrial farming with its high costs of production. It is incapable of producing safe, culturally appropriate, tasty, quality food. And it is incapable of producing enough food for all because it is wasteful of land, water and energy. Industrial agriculture uses ten times more energy than it produces. It is thus ten times less efficient."

Only a seriously sick culture could countenance such a thing as terminator seeds to prevent others growing food without paying again for new seeds. This is so against nature as to be akin to insanity.

By comparison, the 'Great Mystery' / 'Great Spirit' of the earth based indigenous cultures is seen by them as the Source of All Creation, all of which is alive and has soul. Such an attitude seriously discourages the misuse of animals and counters the idea one can produce more and more stuff without looking at the consequences to our Mother Earth. It encourages the concepts of natural herbal and homeopathic medicine which is designed to stimulate the body's own systems to effect healing rather than send in the guns from outside. Homeopathic pills are diluted to the point where there is 'nothing' in them, just the energy residue that will stimulate the body to do what is required to heal itself.

The indigenous way of life also keeps us in mind that sickness in one individual points to the need to look at potential sickness in the family or group to which this person belongs. Becoming a 'normal' person in a sick culture is hardly a recipe for health.

It comes down to the 'God' you hold as divine and how you 'see' the world. Do you see it as a soulless place of separate objects with a 'God' who is an outsider? Or as an integrated place where all is connected and has soul and God is omni-present everywhere in everything?

How does your 'God' affect how you live?

In the older animist earth-based cultures you find the people living and working in family groups, tribes or compounds, all generations together. In this way of living, old people are naturally included and cared for and children are multi-parented. The idea of homes for old people or sending kids away to boarding school would be laughed at with utter derision as the products of insanity. The nuclear family would be looked at as a very unfortunate and deprived way of having to live.

By contrast, male-monotheism produced a God who is single, male, entirely separate, and far away. This 'God-Chap' is seen to relate through Bible teachings (which I have somewhat re-examined in this book) and male priests who impose the beliefs/dogmas of their church. Male-monotheism leads directly to the male dominated patriarchal nuclear family style of living (eg: the wife = Mrs John Smith) and together with the competitive lifestyle that it spawns and scientific materialist paradigm thinking, we are left with little room for old people and this idea that children benefit from being schooled, often in religious institutions, away from parents. Such methods make it easier to fill their minds with religious dogmas, scare them so sh*tless that they believe and obey for the sake of their souls and an afterlife; keep them within the fold and ensure continuation of the status-quo and make them ready to take up arms and fight for 'God and Empire' when called upon.

This feeling of separation, lack of support and need to push the self forward has led to a life of competitive jobs for a wage/salary and inequality on a massive scale. Like I said before, we'd need four and a half more producing planets if everyone lived like an American – and about three and a half to live like a Brit. I recently read that in America in 2007 the **top one per-cent earned more than 23% of all income** and more than the entire combined income of the bottom 50%. The top **one twelfth of one % 'earn' 12 cents of every dollar earned in America.**

A separated god makes separated people and competitiveness, an integral god(s) promotes integrated people and sharing. Living an integrated life one feels part of; living a separated life one feels the need to compete and prove oneself worthy to be included. In an integrated life one is naturally included and self esteem is so natural you don't even need a word for it. In a separated life, self esteem is constantly challenged by others who doubt their own worth and feel the need to push you down to elevate their fragile selves.

Remember the quote about the aboriginal children who played soccer until the scores were equal? In the integrated life, sharing is natural and equality understood as the essence of the good life. In the Native American culture a person was revered for how much they gave – hence the Potlatch ceremony. (We know it as a 'potluck' where everyone brings to share.) If you gave it all away, you knew others would give to you and there would be no lack. This so terrified the conquering, uncomprehending Europeans that they banned the ceremony. They thought those who gave would then come to them for welfare!

Here is Jamie Sams: (Cherokee / Seneca): From *Sacred Path Cards p314*)

"In the native tradition, no one is ever abandoned, orphaned, or left without food, dwellings or help. The understanding among Native people is that when one shares all that he has in order that the people may live, honor and abundance is brought to the giver. Indians have extended families who adopt many relatives and care for one another. Those who are blessed with possessions and food have always shared with those who are lacking. The Medicine Wheel may turn tomorrow and the ones who are in need today may be blessed with abundance that they may share."

Quite a contrast with much modern life where a person tends to be looked up to according to how much he has sequestered for himself out of the system. But to be fair, some who get rich give to charities and some set them up.

Christian Totalitarianism. No right to question:

For hundreds of years, just questioning the 'Word-of-God' was in itself considered heresy. As with Stalinist Communism, a person had no right to question the orthodoxy, no right to his or her own opinion. It could be highly dangerous to question orthodoxy in the hearing of others let alone publicly. The potential price for doing so was some horrible death, so it's not surprising that the populace was kept under subjection. We know this as Totalitarianism, Fascism, Collectivism or Dictatorship, but in those days it was 'correct religious belief', and all 'good people' adhered strictly to it.

Well they had to, didn't they!

Such a policy brings about a homogenous society and makes it easy to keep order with minimal policing. It's particularly effective when you can get the orthodoxy so strong and the fear element so great that people will put the blame on anyone else just to get the heat off themselves: neighbors will rat on neighbors, bosses on their employees, staff on their employers, children on parents, brothers on sisters and so on. This creates a truly terrible society to live in where no one can trust anyone, but it is the most controllable from the point of view of the dominators. It kills the human spirit, crushes the soul, stifles the emotions and nullifies the ability to think. Manna from heaven for dominator psychopaths.

This from writer/researcher Neil Kramer – The Cleaver, January 2011

"Mass culture is a control mechanism that devalues the individual. It is aimed solely at promoting collectivism. It seeks to enforce the dependence of the individual human on a collective group and the priority of group ideologies over individual life paths. It is, at the base level, the very heart of socialism, communism, fascism and totalitarianism. It employs nationalistic impulses to setup polarities of antagonism that exclusively benefits a set of ruling elites. At the top level, the elites fully comprehend that there are no distinct nations, ideologies or cultural imperatives to speak of. To them, there is only power or no power."

For more than a thousand years orthodox Christians suppressed as much knowledge as they could by burning books. (I can already hear cries for this one to be burned! Those who seek to be dominators always hate truth.) In A.D. 391 the Roman-appointed Bishop Theophilus led a mob into the Serapeum quarter of Alexandria and burned the Alexandrian library. The librarian was a brilliant and beautiful woman named Hypatia, a scholar and teacher of Greek knowledge. Here are some of her words:

"All formal dogmatic religions are fallacious and must never be accepted by self-respecting persons as final.

"Reserve your right to think, for even to think wrongly is better than not to think at all.

"*Fables should be taught as fables, myths as myths, and miracles as poetic fancies. To teach superstitions as truths is a most terrible thing. The child mind accepts and believes them, and only through great pain and perhaps tragedy can he be in after years relieved of them. In fact, men will fight for a superstition quite as quickly as for a living truth — often more so, since a superstition is so intangible you cannot get at it to refute it, but truth is a point of view, and so is changeable.*"

The Christian mob stripped her and carved the flesh off her bones while she was still alive. All in the name of 'God', of course. (In *Christianity: An Ancient Egyptian Religion*, author Ahmed Osman says the library was burned to destroy all records of the actual Egyptian roots of Christianity.) They closed the then equivalent of universities and restricted education to priests and those in the approved (i.e. controllable) occupations. Interestingly, that is a procedure echoed by the Taliban today.

Here, from the fringe of Judaism, is a recent newspaper article about a mega racist and separated version of the God-Chap and the bel-lie-f's that 'He' demands.

"'*The sole purpose of non-Jews is to serve Jews*', according to Rabbi Ovadia Yosef, the head of Shas's Council of Torah Sages and a senior Sephardi adjudicator.

'*Goyim were born only to serve us. Without that, they have no place in the world — only to serve the People of Israel,*' he said in his weekly Saturday night sermon on the laws regarding the actions non-Jews are permitted to perform on Shabbat. According to Yosef, the lives of non-Jews in Israel are safeguarded by divinity to prevent losses to Jews.

'*In Israel, death has no dominion over them... .. With gentiles, it will be like any person — they need to die, but [God] will give them longevity. Why? Imagine that one's donkey would die, they'd lose their money. This is his servant. That's why he gets a long life, to work well for this Jew,'* Yosef said.

'Why are gentiles needed? They will work, they will plow, they will reap. We will sit like an effendi and eat. That is why gentiles were created,' he added."

Hilarious – only not funny when you consider he meant it. (I am assuming it is not a spoof.)

So now let's pose the **Magic Question**: *What does (your) God create the universe out of?*

I have been told, "The ether," "He just does … out of nothing," and "He doesn't need anything to create out of."

Okay, so if 'He' creates out of 'nothing,' where is God now?

And, if He creates out of the ether, who was around before to create the ether? A more primal God must have been around first, so he isn't the real god at all.

If you think this through, God the True-ALL-MIGHTY can only create out of Him/Her/It-Self. For God to be ALL-MIGHTY and ABSOLUTE, there can be no thing, no energy, no consciousness, no one and nothing else in existence – or by definition, s/he/it isn't All-Mighty! Now when you read Genesis, from Chapter 2 onwards you find there were lots more people around than just the ones in the 'Garden of Eden'. Cain even went off and married one. So it is absolutely clear that the God-Chap-Jehovah is just a minor bit-player and, judging by his evident bad temper, not even mighty never mind all-mighty.

The real God creates out of Him/Her/Itself and once you understand that the Real God can only create creation out of Its-Self because that is All-There-Is, then you realize that:

God is what we live in and what lives through us.

There is no separation between Creator and Creation

God is The Creation. God is Everything Everywhere –

And you and I live inside God!

And that changes everything! Volumes of complicated 'theology' – like all that Arius vs Athanasius stuff trying to prove whether Jesus is or isn't god or is equal or not quite equal and all that – can go in the garbage can!

It's the blood of the ancients

That flows through our veins

The forms change

But the circle of life remains....

Now how about the following as an example of the religious desire to suppress open investigation into the truth:

The imbeciles vs the Nincompoops:

I watched on TV this most extraordinary debate going on in the USA between those in favor of Darwin and his scientific ideas of evolution and those who want to bring back the God-chap and say that the Universe was 'Intelligently Designed' by this chap in 4004 BC, an extraordinary contradiction in itself!

Well, if I say I'm 'not impressed,' will you fill in the unprintable blanks for me? I watched this BBC Horizon TV program and felt as if I was back in a dark age.

First of all, is there any sensible person anywhere out there who thinks the universe is created *unintelligently?* That the incredible way it all works is some sort of cosmic accident? Or that it 'just happened'? That it is a purposeless, Matrix-like computer game some crazy cosmic unidentified lunatic is play-ing at our expense? If you do think that, look in a mirror to see a nincompoop.

Now, a little history. Darwin's theory of evolution (*Origin of Species*, 1859) shattered the Bible beliefs of that time and so was seen as questioning the very existence of the God-Chap. In the 19th century, religion was weaker than it used to be, so they couldn't burn Darwin as a heretic or even burn all his books, and they rather lost out as Darwin's ideas gradu-ally became the orthodoxy in schools. Now we are witnessing a backlash as the Bible-people want to restore their chap to his former dominance and reduce children to a state of mal-leable ignorance. As per this from James Dobson in *Children at Risk: The Battle for the Hearts and Minds of our Kids* (World Publishing, 1990, p.35):

"Children are the prize in the second great civil war. Those who control what young people are taught and what they experience – what they see, hear, think, and believe – will determine the future course for the nation."

Translation: Whoever can brainwash our kids controls the future.

No wonder there is such a row going on about how Creation is taught in schools. They think kids are stupid enough to believe what they are told in school? May our kids forever be bright enough to think for themselves and foil any such idiocy!

According to the TV program, the religionists came up with a thing called a 'flagellum' that they said could not be reduced to its component parts. This was supposed to 'prove' that the God-Chap had personally created it, hence 'proving,' they said, (with monumental stupidity) the theory of 'Intelligent Design' and making Darwin no longer correct so he could be banished out of schools and replaced by Bible dogma. Well, hard as they tried, inevitably some scientist came up with the answer they didn't want and showed that the jolly flagellum is just like everything else and is developed out of smaller bits that have been around long before.

The whole debate is so ridiculous that I sat there wondering what small percentage of humans are actually intelligent. I felt I was watching imbeciles debating with nincompoops. (That's my printable way of saying it) Rather than intelligent design of the cosmos, how about some simple intelligence amongst humans?

How can the Universe not be intelligently designed when it is so intelligent? The innate intelligence that is in the Universe is itself the intelligence of God, of Creation. When scientists and biologists study the workings of the Universe, they are studying the workings of God. When quantum physicists study the particles and waves that make up the fabric of the manifest Universe, they are studying the inner fabric of God; when astrophysicists study the workings of the stars and galaxies, they are studying the outer fabric of God. When psychologists study the inner workings of a human being, they are studying the workings of God embodied into an individual self-reflective being who is not yet fully conscious of who s/he is. There is no problem until you try to separate God and the Universe, as if the Universe is something separate that some God-Chap did or didn't create. (I used the word 'God' here but you may prefer 'Spirit' or 'Source'. It is the concept that's important, not the specific word.)

Darwin may well be wrong, too, as it seems human bones have been discovered alongside dinosaur bones, so the human race may well be far older than generally thought. (Remember the quote from Professor Dan Smail in Chapter 1) We may even be a genetically created species by the 'sky-gods' coming down and mating with the 'daughters of the earth.' *(See appendix for works of Christian O'Brien and Zecharia Sitchin)* I do not pretend to know, but one thing is sure: current consensus thinking is bunk! We have an enormous amount to discover about our real history, and only a total brainwashed imbecile idiot could think some God-Chap created it all in seven days in 4004 BC! Just as idiotic as the old belief in a flat earth.

We have seen just how much of religious 'orthodoxy' is pure made up manipulation for political ends. So let us come to the real nature of God, and to do this we return to the very beginning where I commented in Chapter I on the change of voice between the two creation stories in Genesis. In the first story-myth, God creates everything in the order it obviously was created in, and man is born of woman. In the second upside down story, a quite different 'God-Chap' appears who interacts with humans, spends most of his time angry, is amazingly vengeful and belligerent, kills just for the hell of it, condemns anyone he doesn't like to eternal torment, and shows himself to be most UNgodly. The majority of the Bible seems to be about this latter chap and misses spirituality, love, care, respect and even bodily hygiene. How on earth have so many people believed this stuff for so long? And isn't it totally amazing that some still do, in this the 21st century?

It doesn't have to be that way. Here is a quote from *Care of the Soul* by Thomas Moore, (Piatkus Books, 1992, pp229)

"The history of our century has shown the proclivity of neurotic spirituality toward psychosis and violence. Spirituality is powerful and therefore has the potential force for evil, as well as for good. The soul needs spirit, but our spirituality also needs soul — deep intelligence, a sensitivity to the symbolic and metaphoric life, genuine community, and attachments to the world.

"We have no idea yet of the positive contribution that could be made to us individually and socially by a more soulful religion and theology. Our culture is in need of theological reflection that does not advocate a particular tradition, but tends the soul's need for spiritual direction. In order to accomplish this goal, we must bring soul back to religion, following Jung, who wrote in a letter of 1910 to Freud, 'What infinite rapture and wantonness lie dormant in our religion. We must bring to fruition its hymn of love.'"

Well, yes, great, such possibility.... But not if we collectively continue to worship (by 'His' own words as shown in Chapter 4) a vicious, angry, intolerant, devious, violent, bigoted, racist, psychopathic, paranoid, schizophrenic, murderous, misogynistic, homophobic, domineering egotist who favors rape of young girls and slavery – and call him our 'God.' That, at the very least, is surely a massive insult to Infinite-Creator-Creation. It also says an uncomfortable lot about the state of human intelligence.

We become what we worship. If we worship a deity of love, compassion and cooperation, we will be able to embrace that as a way of life. If we worship the 'god' described above, it is natural for us to embrace 'His' way of life which is what we've got. Sadly, it is what is considered normal at this time.

Where I sit is holy
Holy is the ground
Rocks and trees and mountains
Listen to their sound
Great Spirit circles
Around me.

Chapter 10
The Hoax of Bible Belief

In the ways of the ancient cultures, it was understood that God – the underlying creative force of the world – was expressed in nature, so if one wanted to learn about God, one studied nature. Remember nature includes everything that exists. It was by observation and study of 'what is' that our ancestors figured out how things are. They did not turn these findings into rigid belief systems that had to be defended against other ideas but rather treated them as understandings that could be deepened as more knowledge became revealed. Here is another quote from Thom Hartmann in *The Last Hours of Ancient Sunlight:*

"Older cultures, with few exceptions, hold as their most founda-tional concept the belief (I prefer the word knowledge) *that we are not different from, separate from, in charge of, superior to, or inferior to the natural world. We are part of it.* **Whatever we do to nature we do to ourselves.***"* (My emphasis)

Looked at in this light, it is amazing that we have replaced such ancient wisdom with belief in a 'Bible' full of extraordi-nary contradictions and a concept of a 'God' that is warlike and bloodthirsty, so far from an expression of love, light and truth. This is mirrored in the culture of wars, of domination of the many by the few; 'ownership' of vast amounts of land and wealth by a relative few; millions starving while food is wasted and dumped; pollution and global warming; a crazy sex 'indus-try' (what a contradiction that is!) fuelled by all the frustra-tion and guilt promoted for centuries by patriarchal religions; trillions spent on 'defense' against other 'ourselves'; weapons of mass destruction which, if used, will terminate a substantial mass of humanity and ravage our planet.

If anyone feels they can convince me we live in a sane world and not an asylum, please go ahead and try. Meanwhile here are some more devastating conclusions from Acharya S. (The Christ Conspiracy p 415.)

"In reality, Christianity was the product of a multinational cabal composed of members of a variety of brotherhoods, secret societies, and mystery schools, and was designed to empower and enrich such individuals and to unify their empire. To do so, these conspirators took myriad myths and rituals of virtually all the known cultures and combined them into one, producing a god-man to beat them all. This unreachable fictional character had since been considered the 'greatest man who ever walked the earth,' to whom no one else can compare and besides whom no one else deserves much recognition and appreciation. All others are, in fact, pathetic born-in-sin wretches. But he did not walk the earth, and we must hereafter allow the dignity of sanctity to be bestowed upon not just one 'man' but all of creation."

And Lloyd Graham writing in *Deceptions and Myths of the Bible* (Citadel, 1991):

*"Such a story as the gospels tell us is unworthy of man's respect; it is, we repeat, the **greatest fraud and hoax ever perpetrated upon mankind.**"*

And from physicist – Hugh Jones (June 2010)

"The greatest threat to mankind comes from religion and its associated medieval philosophies."

Fraud and hoax:

So looking at this from a more personal level, how has it hurt and damaged individuals of the present time? Ask yourself, how has it hurt and damaged you? Are there beliefs you still hold, perhaps subconsciously, that limit, control and impoverish you?

What beliefs do many people hold that keep their souls crushed so much smaller than they could be? What hardships and misery has this fraud brought to masses of people over the last millennias? What are the deep seated anguish and neuroses of the cultures that still live under the brainwashed belief in the God-Chap, under the myth of expulsion from the Garden of Eden, with guilt for being a sexual being and being less than 'Jesus'?

The first is **lousy self-esteem**. I have heard that the Dalai Lama, when addressing a meeting of American Psychotherapists, asked them for the prime reason people sought their services. Their reply was: 'lack of self-esteem.' The Dalai Lama's response was 'What's that?'

Not all cultures suffer the same problems, but how can people of a culture that holds a collective belief of rejection by its God, expulsion out of its God's Garden and being born in sin, possibly hold themselves in esteem? No way! So the first pain of Christianized people is directly the result of cockeyed religious teaching. If you feel deep down that you are unworthy, rejected and abandoned by God, what do you do? The chances are one of three things.

1. Live in your head avoiding emotional pain, rationalizing, logicalizing, and then competing or warring against others to 'prove' yourself.

2. Live destructively with drugs, indulgence, unloving sex, fights and so on.

3. Become a fundamentalist clinging for dear life to The Group who are RIGHT and have the ONLY TRUTH. Perhaps you'll even fantasize the 'rapture' when you will be amongst the 'CHOSEN ONES' and you'll go straight to 'heaven, '*do not*

pass Go, do not collect $200! ... (as they say in the Monopoly game) – *and won't that just show 'em!* (Says your ego loudly.)

The second big issue is **fear.** Again, the teaching that one should 'fear God' is a travesty. Respect the enormity and power of existence – yes – but don't live in fear of it! Fear the result of one's own and others egotism and selfishness – yes. Fear the periodic eruptions of nature – yes. And fear the world-dominating antics of the 'true believers' of the Imposter-God-Chap most of all.

The third is the **defiling and denigration of woman** and the imbalance created between the rights of women and men. Not only has woman has been made a second class citizen, and in some times and places, more like a chattel for the use and abuse of men, but the feminine itself has been denied, denigrated, diminished, disempowered and humiliated to a point of almost being disappeared under the dominance of the male principle.

The fourth is **shame and guilt.** The absurd teachings of the Biblical God-Chap that the body is an unworthy and unholy vehicle for spirit leads to inner war, yourself against yourself. The insane anti-sexual teachings make any normal person feel shame and guilt just because they are normal, as I hope I have shown graphically in earlier chapters.

The fifth is **belief.** As I wrote earlier, just look at the word itself: Be-**LIE**-F. I say: *Belief / disbelief – the closed mind – is the greatest enemy of knowledge.*

And I am not alone in this:

"The greatest enemy of the truth is not lies but firmly held beliefs."

— Schopenhauer

"Belief, in fact, is every human's greatest foe. More people have believed what life is than people who have learned what life is." — Hyemeyohsts Storm, *Lightningbolt* (pp267)

'The devil,' in the shape of people without integrity, is out there in myriad disguises saying believe-in-me, trust-in-us, give us your power, let me make up your mind for you, let me sign your cheques or better still just give me your chequebook to look after; believe in me – a spiritual master – worship at my one true altar; the 'only son of god' is our property and unless you believe what we say, worship with us, you are doomed; we are 'God's Holy Chosen People' and anyone who crosses us is an Enemy of God (so convenient); we bring the 'One True God' to the heathens and until they are converted, they are subhuman so it is our right and duty to conquer them, take their lands, steal their wealth, enslave them and 'save' them – all for their own good, of course.

Belief has been peddled in so many ways but if you make belief superior to knowledge, it beggars any possibility of real understanding, growth and wisdom. The very act of 'becoming a believer' is an act of putting yourself 'in-a-lie', of saying. 'I will close my mind to any further information and hold to this dogma I have chosen to accept'. Believing without knowledge is the real meaning of 'selling your soul to the devil.' It gives you the poison of 'absolute certainty' from which you can attack and denigrate all who see differently.

This poisonous certainty, this 'being-in-the-lie' prevents any connection with real Creator-Creation within which we and all living things exist as co-creators, as aspects of Creation. The price is nothing less than your freedom – and people everywhere seem to be looking for something or someone to pay this diabolical price to. Someone in authority who will tell them what to do, to save them from the deeply humbling journey to self-knowledge; the enormous challenge of self-responsibility; of making and standing by their own choices and reaping the benefits or otherwise; the right and responsibility to create and live their own lives in their own way; the right to explore and learn through experience what really is and is not.

You might feel I am against religion – which is true – but religion is a symptom, it is not the problem itself. The problem is the extraordinary readiness of much of the human race to 'BE-IN-THE-LIE' – the propensity we have to believe what we are told, to take on board what authority figures tell us, to be vulnerable to advertising, coercion, persuasion – in a word: brainwashing. Remember the words of Goebbels I quoted in chapter 1:

'If you tell a lie big enough and keep repeating it, people will eventually come to believe it.'

And remember the willingness of Abraham to tie his own son Isaac to a fire to burn him when 'the lord' told him to..

When a religion is forced on us with the aid of threats to our lives, as happened around AD 300-AD 500 and onward, when the burgeoning cult of Christianity turned ancient myth into literal 'fact' and was then 'nationalized' by the emperor Constantine, it was only too easy for humans to take it on board without too much in the way of thought or reflection. It was either that or being vulnerable to confiscation of your property, being made stateless, or simply being murdered. Then, as time went by, it became accepted as the norm and now millions still 'be-in-the-lie' of it, the torturous and murderous coercion of its origins having been long lost to memory. Take a look at this astonishing experiment: –

Milgram's Experiment on Obedience to Authority:

"Why is it so many people obey when they feel coerced? Social psychologist Stanley Milgram researched the effect of authority

on obedience. He concluded people obey either out of fear or out of a desire to appear cooperative—even when acting against their own better judgment and desires. Milgram's classic yet controversial experiment illustrates people's reluctance to confront those who abuse power.

Milgram recruited subjects for his experiments from various walks in life. Respondents were told the experiment would study the effects of punishment on learning ability. They were offered a token cash award for participating. Although respondents thought they had an equal chance of playing the role of a student or of a teacher, the process was rigged so all respondents ended up playing the teacher. The learner was an actor working as a cohort of the experimenter.

'Teachers' were asked to administer increasingly severe electric shocks to the "learner" when questions were answered incorrectly. In reality, the only electric shocks delivered in the experiment were single 45-volt shock samples given to each teacher. This was done to give teachers a feeling for the jolts they thought they would be discharging.

Shock levels were labeled from 15 to 450 volts. Besides the numerical scale, verbal anchors added to the frightful appearance of the instrument. Beginning from the lower end, jolt levels were labeled: 'slight shock,' 'moderate shock,' 'strong shock,' 'very strong shock,' 'intense shock,' and 'extreme intensity shock'. The next two anchors were 'Danger: Severe Shock', and, past that, a simple but ghastly 'XXX'.

In response to the supposed jolts, the 'learner' (actor) would begin to grunt at 75 volts; complain at 120 volts; ask to be released at 150 volts; plead with increasing vigor, next; and let out agonized screams at 285 volts. Eventually, in desperation, the learner was to yell loudly and complain of heart pain.

At some point the actor would refuse to answer any more questions. Finally, at 330 volts the actor would be totally silent — that is, *if any of the teacher participants got so far without rebelling first. Teachers were instructed to treat silence as an incorrect answer and apply the next shock level to the student.*

If at any point the innocent teacher hesitated to inflict the shocks, the experimenter would pressure him to proceed. Such demands would take the form of increasingly severe statements, such as 'The experiment requires that you continue '."

From Gregorio Billikopf Encina, University of California.

Out of 40 subjects, all continued until the pounding began when five refused to continue. Nine more stopped during the next four questions but twenty-six continued right through 'intense shock', 'danger', 'severe shock' to the maximum XXX. Most subjects started out confident but gradually become distressed, sweating, groaning, complaining, yet continuing.

Milgram reflects:

"Each individual possesses a conscience which, to a greater or lesser degree, serves to restrain the unimpeded flow of impulses destructive to others. But when he merges his person into an **organisational structure***, a new creature replaces autonomous man, unhindered by the limitations of individual morality, freed of humane inhibition, mindful only of the sanctions of authority."*

Astonishing! But that is how dictators of all kinds survive and thrive. Automatic belief in authority is a human trait that we need to work to change. We need to take our individual power back from such habitual patterns of disempowerment that have been deeply ingrained in our ancestors and through them into us. It is part of the cultural consensus norms of society for many generations. Many beliefs are just deeply ingrained stimulous-response patterns.

Let me give you a simple example of a long held belief pattern that is way past its sell-by date: **'Fish on Fridays'.**

Remember that? It was gospel when I grew up that godly people should eat fish on Fridays. Why? History shows that a church document of the Council of Toledo decreed in the year A.D. 447 that believers should abstain primarily from meat on all Fridays and on days of penance.

Then in 1563, *"for the increase of provision of fish by the more usual and common eating thereof,"* it was enacted that, under penalty of a fine or three months jail, fish should be the Friday meal. So because long, long ago fishermen were having a tough time selling their fish, everyone "of faith" had to eat fish on Fridays, *by papal decree!* Canon 1251 of the 1983 Code of Canon Law prescribes: *"abstinence from meat unless a solemnity should fall on a Friday."*

And I can attest that this idea was still prevalent in the nineteen forties and fifties in England when I was growing up. And all because many centuries ago fishermen were having a hard time selling fish!

Now here is a much more horrendous result of 'being-in-the-lie':

Female genital mutilation is an appalling, torturous, agonizing, invasive and destructive procedure that is part of many North and West African cultures and also some South American ones too. It predates the religions we know and to their lasting shame, neither Christianity nor Islam have made any attempt to prevent it. It is usually forced on girls before puberty. Part, or all, of the clitoris is cut out and in the most extreme cases the labia are sewn up with just a small hole for menstrual blood to escape. All without anaesthetic, until recently. This is an incredible trauma and it leaves women with reduced or no sexual feeling. Orgasms are often impossible to experience and many health and psychological problems result from the 'surgery'. Death has been quite a common result.

Here is one unfortunate woman's experience verbatim:

"I was seven years old when I was excised. I recall the stories from women of my village who spoke of this operation as if their whole life had stopped there and then. The atrocity of their descriptions and at the same time a feeling of inescapable doom had triggered such a panic in me that when the terror-laden day came, I began to vomit. What happened then is still excruciatingly burning my flesh, so much so that I often wake up in the middle of the night screaming and calling for my mother."

The horrible irony to that is that her mother will have been fully complicit in the terror and pain she experienced, as it is the women who, generation by generation, do it to the women. I watched a TV program here in UK about three years ago which showed it being done on two girls somewhere in Africa. It was done with a local anaesthetic (imagine having a needle thrust into the tenderest part of your genitals) yet it was unbelievably horrendous, especially seeing the mounting terror of the second girl to be 'done' as she saw what was happening as her sister was held down by several large women, forced into submission and then cut. It was quite dreadful to watch but I wanted to know the truth.

Some say this practice comes from the Egyptian Pharaohs. (See *Women of Omdurman* by Anne Cloudsley and '*Do they hear you when you cry?*' by Fauziya Kassindja. Details in Resources) I have been unable to find out its origins but there is one thing I can say for certain. It comes from patriarchy, from male domination and the desire of some males to reduce women to mere chattels for their pleasure and service.

I read that this operation is still forced on approximately 6,000 girls per day worldwide – about one every 15 seconds. It is time for a serious campaign of education to help those who are still robotically committing this appalling act because of their 'be-**lie**-fs.'

Orthodoxies and the penalties of thinking for yourself:

There is another effect of our readiness to fall into consensus beliefs. If you dare to think for yourself and challenge orthodoxies such as current scientific orthodoxy about global warming and climate change for example; or if you challenge medical orthodoxy about cancer treatment or vaccination, you are liable to lose your job or your funding. In extremis, if you threaten loudly the profits of large corporations with entrenched profit lines and resources to burn, you may end up barred from practicing your profession or even in jail.

It is important to remember that all new inventions, paradigm shifts and radical changes in world view are achieved by mavericks and not by followers of orthodoxies. Jesus (whoever he may or may not have been) was not a Christian, Buddha was not a Buddhist, Jung was not a Jungian and Freud was not a Freudian, Newton was not a Newtonian, Einstein was not an Einsteinian, and so it goes. All great and small new insights, realizations, creations are the product of courageous people who dared to think and act outside the box. Mavericks, not followers.

In the words of William Blake: "*I must create my own system or be enslaved to another man's. My business is not to reason and compare. It is to create.*"

There is another thing too, in present time: In my own profession of healing/spirituality/psychotherapy etc. there has recently come about a plethora of regulation and the idea that everyone should be 'qualified'. Now look at the word 'qualification'. Oxford dictionary: "*Modification, recognition of contingency, restricting or limiting circumstance. Quality fitting person or thing, condition that must be fulfilled before right can be acquired or office held.*" It is all about limiting, restricting and controlling.

There are therapy training courses galore and I have even come to include practitioner training in my own prospectus. But there is a joke hidden behind all that. Just like the prominent figures mentioned above, the creators of the disciplines people avidly train in were never qualified themselves! How could they be? The disciplines didn't exist until they invented them! They were mavericks who thought outside boxes, usually to the great benefit of the human race. (In my own work I make sure participants understand that whatever they learn through my work, it is for them to put their own knowledge and insight together in their own unique way.)

There is another interesting issue here too. Who knows if a healer / doctor / therapist / teacher is any good? It isn't the bureaucracy, it isn't an organizer or anyone in sat an office doing paperwork. The only people who know are the clients, patients, students or participants, the recipients of the treatment! No amount of paper qualifications can make a duff worker any good and no lack of them can prevent a genius from being brilliant!

Here is **Buddha on what to believe – and what not to believe:**

Do not believe in anything simply because you have heard it.

Do not believe in anything simply because it is spoken and rumored by many.

Do not believe in anything simply because it is found written in your religious books.

Do not believe in anything merely on the authority of your teachers and elders. Do not believe in traditions because they have been handed down for many generations.

But after observation and analysis, when you find that anything agrees with reason and is conducive to the good and benefit of one and all, then accept it and live up to it.

All that we are is the result of what we have thought. If a man speaks or acts with an evil thought, pain follows him. If a man speaks or acts with a pure thought, happiness follows him, like a shadow that never leaves him.

Like I said earlier, Buddhism is not a religion, it is a path. A path is something shown to us by wise ancestors and wise elders who indicate the way and guide us towards knowing our-self.

But The Path is something each of us walks alone....

Chapter 11
The Cosmic Asylum?

It sometimes feels to me as if this planet is a giant Cosmic therapy group – or even asylum – for wayward souls who have been sent here from more advanced cultures in the Universe to sort ourselves out! We are given amazing opportunities to screw up all over the place, incredible selfless service from all the other kingdoms, and constant feedback of the consequences of our actions. Only if we mess up the whole planet will we bring this opportunity to a close. Graduation is what we know as 'enlightenment'.

Right about now, we've reached a highly critical situation. Here are some words from a very knowledgeable person: Erwin Laszlo, Ph.D., founder and president of The Club of Budapest, founder and director of the General Evolution Research Group, and editor of the international periodical *World Futures*, as well as author of 47 books. (Writing in *Caduceus Magazine*, Spring 2006)

"We are approaching a critical point in our collective evolution: our world has become economically, socially and ecologically unsustainable. Persisting in the values and practices of the rationalistic, manipulative civilization of the modern age will create deepening rifts between rich and poor, young and old, informed and marginalized, and human societies and the natural environment. To survive in our planetary home, we must create a world better adapted to the conditions we have ourselves created."

And this from an African tribal shaman (with two PhDs) about our current situation.

"There is no doubt that, at this moment in history, Western Civilization is suffering from a great sickness of the soul. The West's progressive turning away from functioning spiritual values; its

total disregard for the environment and the protection of natural resources; the violence of inner cities with their problems of poverty, drugs and crime; spiraling unemployment and economic disarray; and growing intolerance toward people of color and values of other cultures — all of these trends, if unchecked, will eventually bring about a terrible self-destruction. In the face of all this global chaos, the only possible hope is self-transformation."

— Malidoma Patrice Some, PhD, PhD, Dagara Shaman from Burkina Faso. From *'Of Water and the Spirit'*.

Exactly! – Self-Transformation! Not infantile beliefs that some 'God-Chap' or 'His Son' will do it all for you.

And this from writer/teacher Andrew Harvey:

"The facts of our global crisis, a crisis at once political and economic, psychological and environmental, show us clearly that the human race has no hope of survival unless it chooses to undergo a total transformation, a total change of heart. What is required is a massive and quite unprecedented spiritual transformation. There is no precedent for what we are being asked to do. **Only the leap into a new consciousness can engender the vision, the moral passion, the joy and energy necessary to effect change on the scale and with the self-sacrifice that is essential to save (our presence on) the planet in the time we have left.** *Catastrophe can become grace, and disaster possibility, only if we transform their energy by accepting what they have to teach us and acting with complete sincerity to transform ourselves."* (My emphasis added)

2012 is almost here and the Mayan Calendar and many other long term cycles come to a point around this time suggesting great change is approaching. Many challenges are coming our way both collectively and individually. Each of us will have to choose whether we stand for the good of all or just for self.

Here are a few reflections on how we are currently doing. In the USA, the richest country in the world: –

* *1 in 6 children has a neuro-developmental disorder.*

* *14% of American children today are enrolled in a learning disability program.*

* *There are between 2 and 4 million autistic children in the U.S. today whereas in 1990 there were practically none.*

* *The number of children with allergies has doubled in the past 11 years.*

* *The rate of childhood cancer is increasing at an exponential rate to levels never seen before or imagined.*

* *According to the CDC, 60% of children in the US are overweight or obese.*

* *Autoimmune diseases, diabetes, asthma, MS and brain tumors among young people are skyrocketing.*

From *Vaccination is not immunization* by Dr Tim O'Shea. Highly recommended. (Sorry, I don't have stats for UK or Europe.)

A few more statistics which show the craziness of modern ways. From *Rogue Nation* by Vernon Coleman (Blue Books):

"It is now claimed that 200,000 Americans get food poisoning every day. Modern processed meats are said to leave more fecal bacteria on the average American kitchen sink than can be found on the average American toilet seat."

JAMA (the Journal of the American Medical Association) estimates that in one year well over two million hospitalized patients in the USA have serious Adverse Drug Reactions, while 106,000 have fatal ones. In fact, **it is between the 4th and 6th leading cause of death in USA!**

Every year around 100,000 Americans die of infections caught in hospital. Many British, too.

Another source says a total of 350,000 Americans die per annum (2005) from both properly and improperly prescribed medications and that it is now **the 3rd leading cause of death.**

It seems that boys in American schools who run about and shout tend to be diagnosed as hyperactive! It has been claimed that up to **12 % of all American boys of age 6-14 are on Ritalin or similar drugs!**

From Wall Street Journal, December 2010: *'These days, the medicine cabinet is truly a family affair. More than a quarter of U.S. kids and teens are taking a medication on a chronic basis, according to Medco Health Solutions Inc., the biggest U.S. pharmacy-benefit manager with around 65 million members. Nearly 7% are on two or more such drugs, based on the company's database figures for 2009'.*

Our appetites are betraying us. The most popular beverage in the world carries a label on its side that basically declares it to have no nutritional value whatsoever!

The 'Codex Alimentaris' now being touted for law by the 'Church of Big Pharma' across the USA and Europe wants to stop many herbal/natural remedies being sold. Sadly for them, drug companies can't make profits from natural remedies that cannot be patented.

Note this: Deaths in the US through patent medicines in 2008 = 106,000

Deaths through vitamins / supplements / herbal products / homeopathic remedies = zero.

Sports stars, pop stars and entertainers (inspirational – yes, but upon whom little of major consequence depends) are paid in millions. Recently also 'banksters' who do 'clever' dodges with paper money while producing nothing consumable. Meanwhile teachers, agricultural workers, engineers, nurses, police, firemen, librarians and similar (to say nothing of Mothers) upon all of whom much of consequence depends – scrape by on modest salaries.

(It's just been in the news that Barclays Bank in UK is paying its CEO £27 million and its two highest paid 'geniuses' – the aptly named Rich Ricci £44 million and someone with a less memorable name £47 million. This is a sick joke. How many times more is that than the minimum wage? My back of envelope calculation comes to around 3800 times. That is inequality gone rampant. It simply cannot last.

They say they have to pay these sums to compete in the market for people of such 'ability'. The ability reflected in their share price? Down from over £60 in 2007 to under £20 now. Doesn't it make you feel that we're being conned? How come all these people are 'worth' so much?

Tower Hamlets, where Barclays HQ is situated, is one of the poorest boroughs in London. A group of teachers complained that the bonus pool of £3.5 billion paid to Barclays employees was more than has been spent on education in the borough in the past ten years.)

The USA is reckoned to be responsible for a quarter of all pollution on the planet. China and the industrial nations of the Far East are catching up fast as they are copying the unsustainable lifestyles of the West. How sad is this?

Here is a shocking world statistic: 800 million people are malnourished, six million die each year for lack of basic necessities, and one child starves to death every five seconds. Yet huge food surpluses are regularly destroyed, callously ignoring the many thousands around the world who go to bed hungry each night.

The Empire delusion:

Many male animals live in a 'f*ck-or-fight' universe, one of simple power over others, of territorial battles. However these battles are usually resolved by either shows of strength or battles between two competing alpha males. We humans have taken this to an horrendous extreme and battle each other with vast armies and weapons of mass destruction causing death and misery on a vast scale. We have created empire after empire based on just such narrow thinking. It is worthwhile noting that *every empire*, all the way from Gilgamesh to the British Empire, *has fallen!* The current 'emperors' – the Americans – are clearly approaching the end of their time right now and have been behaving with reckless abandon in their death throes, as did many empires before.

For all our advancement in the ways of science and the manipulation of material things, we are still, very sadly, an ignorant species as regards knowledge of ourselves and we are an enormously long way from learning to live in co-operation and harmony with each other and our planet. We are still primitive, territorial and warlike. We have yet to develop a working-together global consciousness and it is dubious whether we will be able to do that before our destruction of the ecology of the earth dooms a large number of us to an early and unnecessary demise. This is the biggest challenge of the 21st century.

War and Money:

Here's some scary stuff from financial expert Clif Droke, (www.clifdroke.com):

"... it has long been known by our nation's leaders that war is primarily a tool for achieving economic gain and not, as in the days of old, for territorial gains. Senator John M. Thurston of Nebraska made this infamous statement just before the Spanish American War: **'War with Spain would increase the business and earnings of every American railroad, it would increase the output of every American factory, it would stimulate every branch of industry and domestic commerce.'**

"More recently, to end the 2000-2003 bear market and recession it was deemed necessary for the U.S. to invade Afghanistan and Iraq. Although these actions were successful in lifting the U.S. from its financial malaise, it also had the spin-off effect of escalating commodities prices, particularly the above mentioned metals and petroleum prices. This leads us to the conundrum of **how the current inflationary environment will be addressed by the financial controllers. Specifically, will it require a further escalation of military activities (war with Iran?)** Or will it require a respite in military activities for a while and a corresponding slowdown in money creation to temporarily cool off commodities prices?

Interesting about the Iraq war:

"In 2003 the UN didn't need to send weapons inspectors into Iraq to find out what weapons Saddam Hussein had. All the UN needed to do was to ask the British and American Governments for an inventory. It was the British and American Governments who provided Iraq with its weapons. (Some had been gifts and some had been sold.)"

"We can say unequivocally that the industrial infrastructure needed by Iraq to produce nuclear weapons has been eliminated."

- Scott Ritter, Former UN weapons inspector, before the destruction of Iraq. (from *Rogue Nation*)

And more scary – the new doctrine of pre-emptive war:

"This coming battle, if it materializes, represents a turning point in USA foreign policy and possibly a turning point in the recent history of the world. This nation is about to embark upon the first test of a revolutionary doctrine applied in an extraordinary way at an unfortunate time. **The doctrine of pre-emption – the idea that the US or any other nation can legitimately attack a nation that is not imminently threatening but may be threatening in the future** *– is a radical new twist on the traditional idea of self-defense. It appears to be in contravention of international law and the UN charter. And it is being tested at a time of world-wide terrorism, making many countries around the globe wonder if they will soon be on our - or some other nations – hit list."*

— US Senator Robert Byrd, speaking in the USA Senate 12.2.03, (quoted in *Rogue Nation* by Vernon Coleman, Blue Books, 2003.)

Arms and hunger:

Each year the world spends over $1 trillion on arms. The Presidential Commission on World Hunger estimated that it would cost $6 billion per year to eradicate starvation and malnutrition.

That is equivalent to less than three days arms expenditure!

Western world debt:

"According to the Federal Reserve's most recent report on wealth, America's private net worth was $53.4 trillion as of September, 2009. But at the same time, America's debt and unfunded liabilities totalled at least $120,000,000,000,000.00

*($120 trillion), or **225% of the citizens' net worth**. Even if the
government expropriated every dollar of private wealth in the
nation, it would still have a deficit of $66,600,000,000,000.00
($66.6 trillion), equal to $214,286.00 for every man, woman and
child in America and roughly 500% of GDP. If the government does
not directly seize the nation's private wealth, then it will require
$389,610 from each and every citizen to balance the country's
books. State, county and municipal debts and deficits are additional,
already elephantine in many states (e.g., California, Illinois, New
Jersey and New York) and growing at an alarming rate nationwide.
In addition to the federal government, dozens of states are already
bankrupt and sinking deeper into the morass every day."*

So writes Stewart Dougherty - www.kitco.com January
22, 2010

Here is a staggering cover story (*USA Today*, November 14,
2005) quoting David Walker, the ex- US Comptroller General:
*"The United States can be likened to Rome before the fall of the
empire. Its financial condition is 'worse than advertised'... It has a
'broken business model' and faces deficits in its budgets, its balance
of payments, its savings - and its leadership."*

And this from US Senator Ron Paul – January 2010

*"Could it all be a bad dream? Or a nightmare? Is it my imagina-
tion or have we lost our minds? It's surreal; it's just not believable; a
grand absurdity; a great deception of momentous proportions based
on preposterous notions and on ideas whose time should never
have come. Simplicity grossly distorted and complicated; insanity
passed off as logic; grandiose schemes built on falsehoods with the
morality of Ponzi and Madoff; evil described as virtue; ignorance
pawned off as wisdom; destruction and impoverishment in the
name of humanitarianism; violence, the tool of change; preventive
wars used as the road to peace; tolerance delivered by government
guns; reactionary views in the guise of progress; an empire replacing*

the Republic; slavery sold as liberty; excellence and virtue traded for mediocracy; socialism to save capitalism; a government out of control, unrestrained by the Constitution, the rule of law or morality; bickering over petty politics as we collapse into chaos. The philosophy that destroys us is not even defined.

We have broken from reality – a psychotic nation; ignorance with a pretense of knowledge replacing wisdom. Money does not grow on trees, nor does prosperity come from a government printing press or escalating deficits. We're now in the midst of unlimited spending of the people's money, exorbitant taxation, deficits of trillions of dollars spent on a failed welfare/warfare state; an epidemic of cronyism; unlimited supplies of paper money equated with wealth. A central bank that deliberately destroys the value of the currency in secrecy, without restraint, without nary a whimper. Yet cheered on by the pseudo-capitalists of Wall Street, the military-industrial complex and Detroit."

In the UK it is uncomfortably similar:

The UK national debt clock is ticking fast. The Government says our debt will be **£1.216 trillion** by April 2012. It is estimated that with all 'hidden' debts counted including borrowing from the future (ie from our childrens' earnings), the full debt is nearer £4.8 trillion. Yes, that really is £4.800,000,000,000.

To pay last year's **£43 billion** interest bill, every household will stump up more than **£1,800 in tax**. That's not a joke - that really is how much it's going to cost you. The UK's national debt has become so astronomical that it's hard to make sense of it anymore

Average household debt in the UK is approximately **£47,866 including mortgages**. Britain's personal debt is increasing by approx £1 million every four minutes. The government borrows £1 for every £4 it spends.

In the UK economy the public sector which consumes wealth is now larger than the private sector which creates wealth. This is a gigantic long term problem which will take enormous political will to solve.

And from a broader perspective:

"*Whenever destroyers appear among men, they start by destroying money; for money is man's protection and the base of a moral existence. Destroyers seize gold and leave to its owners a counterfeit pile of paper. This kills all objective standards and delivers men into the arbitrary power of an arbitrary setter of values. Gold is an objective value, an equivalent of wealth produced. Paper is a mortgage on wealth that does not exist, backed by a gun aimed at those who are expected to produce it. Paper is a check drawn by legal looters upon an account which is not theirs: upon the virtue of the victims. Watch for the day when it bounces, marked, 'Account Overdrawn.'*"

— Ayn Rand from Atlas Shrugged (1957)

"*The secret of success is to realize that the crisis on our planet is much larger than just deciding what to do with your own life, and if the system under which we live, the structure of western civilization, begins to collapse because of our selfishness and greed, then it will make no difference whether you have $1 million dollars when the crash comes or just $1.00. The only work that will ultimately bring any good to any of us is the work of contributing to the healing of the world.*" Marianne Williamson.

And with a touch of black humor – from financial wiz 'Anonymous'!

"The world will soon wake up to the reality that everyone is broke and can collect nothing from the bankrupt, who are owed unlimited amounts by the insolvent, who are attempting to make late payments on a bank holiday in the wrong country with an unacceptable currency against defaulted collateral of which nobody knows who holds the title!"

Chapter 12
Reflections on the Asylum
and Some Inmates
Who Want To Take Over

*"When I, or people like me, are running the country, you'd better flee, because I will find you, we will try you, and we will execute you. I mean every word of it. I will make it part of my mission to see to it that they are tried and executed …. If we're going to have true reformation in America, it is because men once again, if I may use a worn out expression, have righteous testosterone flowing through their veins. They are not afraid of contempt for their contemporaries. They are not here to get along. **They are here to take over,"***

— Randall Terry, founder of Operation Rescue, addressing a banquet sponsored by the US Tax Payers Alliance, August 8, 1995. (Operation Rescue is a US anti-abortion organization.)

Well, Mr. Terry, that is nice and clear. When you and your kin *take over,* God help the rest of us, we will be back in the Dark Ages and the Unholy Inquisition. This is 21st century America, not Biblical times, and we will not vote you in.

Here he is again, quoted in the *Fort Wayne News Sentinel* of August 16, 1993:

"I want you to just let a wave of intolerance wash over you. I want you to let a wave of hatred wash over you. Yes, hate is good …. Our goal is a Christian nation. We have a Biblical duty; we are called by God to conquer this country."

Sounds just like the Old Testament 'God-Chap', doesn't he? Or some of today's worst Islamic extremists. Just as virulent, foul, bigoted, intolerant, domineering, full of hate and venom. I wonder what sort of love-life and mothering he had that left him hating so much. And isn't that a funny sort of 'Christian Country' he wants? Most Christian people talk about a loving, caring, sharing way of living, even if they are confused that they are supposed to include all people and not just fellow Christians. Still, at least he leaves no doubt about what he's aiming at.

"What you are going to hear is God's word to the men of this nation. We are going to war as of tonight. We have divine power that is our weapon. We will not compromise. Whatever truth is at risk, in the schools or legislature, we are going to contend for it. We will win … Take the nation for Jesus Christ."

— Bill McCartney. (Another right wing protagonist)

Next is a fabulous bit of rationalization from Christian Reconstuctionist Gary North, taken from *The Sinai Strategy: Economics and the Ten Commandments* (p.214):

"It occurs to me: Was Moses arrogant and unbiblical when he instructed the Israelites to kill every Canaanite in the land (Deut 7:2 and 20:16-17. (And see Chapter 4) Was he an elitist or (horror of horrors) a racist? No; he was a God-fearing man who sought to obey God, who commanded them to kill them all. It sounds like a 'superior attitude' to me. Of course, Christians have been given no comparable military command in New Testament terms, but I am trying to deal with the attitude of superiority – a superiority based on our possession of the law of God. That attitude is something Christians must have when dealing with all Pagans. God has given us the tools of dominion."

My God (I invoke the real one, not the imposter God-Chap), that is almost unspeakable in its superior attitude. 'We the Christians have the right to kill who we choose, we have the right to dominion' = domination over everyone else because the God-Chap gave it us. They invent their own 'god' and they 'obey' the monstrous dictates they put in 'his' mouth!

It is like the worst horrors of the Old Testament and the Inquisition coming back to haunt the 21st century.

Here he is again writing in *Backward Christian Soldiers:*

"Christians are supposed to love each other. Communists are supposed to share bonds with all proletarians and other communists. Every ideological group proclaims universality, and all of them bicker internally, never displaying unity except in the face of a common enemy. Humanism today is the common enemy of Christians."

Yes, Christians are supposed to love each other and – if we take the words attributed to their number two God-Chap Jesus seriously – everyone else, too – unconditionally. And yes, every ideological group bickers and guess what – Christians are incredibly good at that, too.

Here is Pat Robertson, – remember him? He ran for president of the USA in 1984, but fortunately lost by so big a margin he didn't try again and nor have any other TV evangelists. Quoted in '700 Club', 1991.

"You say you're supposed to be nice to the Episcopalians and the Presbyterians and the Methodists, and this and that and the other thing. Nonsense, I don't have to be nice to the spirit of the Anti-Christ. I can love the people who hold false opinions, but I don't have to be nice to them."

How many Christian groups are there? I remember reading a figure quoted over 4,800 some years ago. Just as at the beginning with Arius and Athanasius (see Chapter 6) and in the world of Islam with the Sunnis and the Shias, they bicker and make war on each other. Then he calls the humanists the enemy of Christians. Why? Are they not sufficiently brainwashed? Might they talk sense and influence Christians to think for themselves? If too many people actually think for themselves, what future is there for religion?

Here is another revealing piece from *Backward Christian Soldiers*:

"The battle for the mind, some fundamentalists believe, is between fundamentalism and the institutions of the left. This conception of the battle is fundamentally incorrect. The battle for the mind is between the Christian Reconstruction Movement, which **alone among Protestant groups** *takes seriously the Law of God, and everyone else."*

Aah, so it isn't the humanists or even the Catholics who are the real enemy, it's all the other Protestant Christian groups!

"We are to make Bible-obeying disciples of anybody that gets in our way."

So said Jay Grimstead in February 1987, the above quoted in *America's Taliban* by David W Irish, (Highly recommended)

No messing – 'we make them bible-obeying.' The God-Chap's representatives love a bit of force now and again when their god isn't busy telling people to kill each other.

Here is Pat Robertson again *"There will never be world peace until God's house and God's people are given their rightful place of leadership at the top of the world."*

Translation: Until we have got domination and can tell everyone else what to do, we won't let there be any peace.

And to rub it in clearly, he goes on:

"The strategy against the American radical left should be the same as Gen. Douglas MacArthur employed against the Japanese in the Pacific …. Bypass their strongholds, then surround them, isolate them, bombard them, then blast the individuals out of their power bunkers with hand to hand combat. The battle for Iwo Jima was not pleasant but our troops won it. The battle to regain the soul of America won't be pleasant either, but we will win it."

— Pat Robertson's Perspective, April-May 1992.

Translation: We will force our beliefs on America regardless of the cost.

Sounds ever more like the Old Testament. Violence, threat, war, domination, hate, killing .... Is this really what we all want in the 21ˢᵗ century? Is this the loving, caring religion of 'gentle Jesus'? No, it's what is hidden under the surface of the world domination cult of corporate-Christianity. And it is here in the 21ˢᵗ century alive and violently kicking in America today.

More from Pat Robertson

"I know there are some Christians who believe that war and their participation in it are morally wrong. While I respect their views and must allow them to follow their consciences, I do not believe the Bible teaches pacifism."

Well, he is right about that - it doesn't! It teaches war, genocide, murder and slavery as I hope I have made abundantly clear. Here is Robertson on feminism:

Feminism is a socialist, anti-family, political movement that encourages women to leave their husbands, kill their children, practice witchcraft, destroy capitalism and become lesbians.

Well that's new to me. I know a lot of feminists and none of them have killed any children. Some are family people, some are lesbians and some heteros, some are 'wise women' (the real meaning of 'witch'), some are herbalists, homeopaths, doctors, healers of all kinds; some are capitalists and some are socialists. Obviously Robertson lives amongst a uniquely narrow section of society!

Gary North leaves no doubt that he wants to be in control....

"The long term goal of Christians in politics should be to gain **exclusive control over the franchise.** (My emphasis. At least the guy states his agenda clearly, frightening as it is) *Those who refuse to submit publicly to the eternal sanctions of God (that*

means Gary and Co, folks) *by submitting to His Church's* (that's Gary's church, folks) *public marks of the covenant – baptism and holy communion – must be denied citizenship, just as they were in ancient Israel."*

Wow! You can see what would happen if the rightwing Christians really got power in America. Oh, what's that you say? They already did? Mr. G. W. Bush and his crew? Well they are out of office now but there is still a mighty powerful Bible bashing, freedom bashing, lobby.

And here's Gary again advocating a touch of stealth in pushing their agenda:

"So let us be blunt about it: we must **use the doctrine of religious liberty** *to gain independence for Christian schools until we train up a generation of people who know there is no religious neutrality, no neutral law, no neutral education, and no neutral civil government. Then they will get busy in constructing a Bible-based social, political and religious order which* **finally denies the religious liberty** *of the enemies of God."* (Again - my emphasis)

So he wants to use democratic freedom to get power so he can do away with democratic freedom, just like so many scheming dictators and power thirsty psychopaths. And in the words of R.J Rushdooney:

"(We seek to) replace the heresy of democracy with Biblical law."

Rushdooney was a Calvinist (remember Calvin? – see Chapters 3 and 8) and is the 'godfather' of Christian Reconstructionism. (Quote from *America's Taliban*.)

So for this bunch of 'Christians', democracy is a heresy. Well, of course. It stops them taking over and dominating everyone and returning the world to the Dark Ages of ignorance, poverty of spirit, the horrors of Old Testament law, the burning of books, the limitation of knowledge, the crushing of the soul, the forced uniformity of thinking, the brainwashing of the masses, the reduction of everyone else to their level of putrid, pathetic, hate-filled, paranoid, psychopathic existence.

And how about this? They even say Jesus was a killer:

"The significance of Jesus Christ as the 'faithful and true witness' is that He not only witnesses against those who are at war against God, but **He also executes them.**"

Rushdoney in *The Institutes of Biblical Law* (p.574) (also quoted in *America's Taliban*).

And how about this offering from Charles Stanley, the former two-time president of the Southern Baptist Convention and close ally of former President George Bush (senior) and fervent supporter of the war on Iraq:

"The government is **ordained by God** *with the right to promote good and restrain evil. This includes wickedness that exists within the nation, as well as any wicked persons or countries that threaten foreign nations ... Therefore, a government has biblical grounds to go to war in the nation's defense or to liberate others in the world who are enslaved."*

The last sentence is a worthy statement. The problem is who gets to decide what is actually threatening to the nation and what constitutes enslavement of another nation.

Strange isn't it, how it usually seems to rest on how much oil is there....

Stanley warned that those who oppose or disobey the U.S. government in its drive to war *"will receive condemnation upon themselves."*

Stanley is pastor at Atlanta's First Baptist Church, a 15,000-member congregation, and is the founder of In Touch

Ministries, which claims to broadcast his sermons in 14 languages to every country in the world, and which, according to Americans United for Separation of Church and State, has $40 million in assets.

And then this from Becky Fischer, Christian summer camp director, in Jesus Camp (2006)

"It's no wonder, with that kind of intense training and disciplining, that those young people are ready to kill themselves for the cause of Islam. I wanna see young people who are as committed to the cause of Jesus Christ as the young people are to the cause of Islam. I wanna see them as radically laying down their lives for the Gospel as they are over in Pakistan and Israel and Palestine and all those different places, you know, because we have... excuse me, but we have the truth!"

She wants Christians to stoop to the level of Islamic fundamentalists and blow themselves up. If she succeeds maybe they'll have a big party and blow each other up and there will be...? What will be left, I wonder, for those of us who don't want to blow up anyone or anything?

Here is Pat Robertson again, from *The New World Order*, 1991:

"When I said during my presidential bid that I would only bring Christians and Jews into the government, I hit a firestorm. 'What d'you mean?' the media challenged me. 'You're not going to bring atheists into the government? How dare you maintain that those who believe the Judeo-Christian values are better qualified to govern America than Hindus and Muslims?' My simple answer is, 'Yes, they are.'"

Notice how he pits Christians and Jews as believers against Hindus and Moslems as atheists (which they are not), rather than the harder to attack humanitarians and reasonable people who want to keep the separation of church and state so that doctrinaire beliefs are kept out.

And note this, also from Robertson: (Op-Ed column in *USA Today*, June 2, 1994)

*"The First Amendment guarantees freedom **of** religion, not freedom **from** religion."*

Well, that says it all! In America, they have carte blanche to push it down your throat, no matter what! Here is a little piece from *The New World Order* (1991) where, unwittingly, he may have tumbled on a deeper truth:

"Indeed, it may well be that men of goodwill like Woodrow Wilson, Jimmy Carter and George Bush (he means sr.), *who sincerely want a larger community of nations living at peace in our world, are in reality unknowingly and unwittingly carrying out the mission and mouthing the phrases of a tightly knit cabal whose goal is nothing less than a new order for the human race under the domination of Lucifer and his followers."*

New World Order' – 'Illuminati':

There are an increasing number of people who are very concerned that, under all the surface politics, this is exactly what is really happening. We can all see that terrorism is the excuse to vastly increase surveillance on citizens in both America and Britain, and much of Europe too. The horrible Orwellian vision many concerned people have is that this cabal of mega rich families, usually referred to as the 'Illuminati', will, in years to come, have us all electronically tagged and photographed, create a financial crisis which will enable money to be replaced by 100% electronic, checkable transactions, have us all medicated into a comfortable tranquilized state of semi-consciousness and whose ultimate aim that the human race should live as pawns in a controlled, restricted, overseen, totalitarian one-world state – just like *The Matrix*, only worse. Such a killing of the human spirit is worth struggling against but it is worth reflecting that quite a lot of Europe has already experienced a similar kind of condition when living under the Unholy Inquisition, a little of which I described in the chapter 8. We have already had times like this, only it was not world-wide. And the dominators have nearly lost their greatest tool – religion – which no longer has the god-chap-given right to 'cleanse' the world of those who don't agree with them.

However, the tool they have left is money and they are incredibly rich and are currently printing it with abandon.

"And to what benefit? So that a bunch of pathetic sociopaths can try and fill the hole in their hollow beings with trophy wives and trophy houses, empty titles and hair pieces, extravagant lifestyles with ridiculously overpriced cars and jewelry and ugly art, spoiled idiot children who hate and fear them as they hated and feared their own parents, and the illusion of love and power while making asses out of themselves as a few paid sycophants sing their praises, trodding over corpses on the road to hell."

Words of blogger Jesse. Nail hit firmly on head! (http://jessescrossroadscafe.blogspot.com)

Lastly - the worst nightmare we all face: The 'Rapture' - Armageddon and the most extremist fundamentalist Christians:

The ultimate worst danger to all of us on Earth is posed by those utter abysmal lunatic fanatics who think the God-Chap will bring about a 'Rapture' of all fundamentalist Christians – of their particular sect, of course, no one else – if/when Armageddon comes. The 'Rapture' is the idea that suddenly all 'true believers' (in the 'right beliefs' <u>only</u>, of course) will be bodily lifted off the planet up to 'heaven' while the rest of us are left to burn in whatever shambles is left. This means the believers need have no concern for the welfare of the earth, no concern for the welfare of other humans who don't share their beliefs, no concern for the animals (after all, the religion says they don't have souls), no concern for the plants, insects, indeed for the planet herself. This is the ultimate destructive belief system and represents a considerable danger to the vast majority of us. It is like suicide bombing only on a massive scale. One suicide bomber takes relatively few people, animals and buildings with him, but frightened fundamentalist mani-acs looking for 'rapture' will be content to destroy the whole planet and all the rest of us with it.

And they call their God a Loving God?

To sum up this chapter:

"Our scientific power has outrun our spiritual power. We have guided missiles and misguided men."

— Martin Luther King.

"Today, every inhabitant of this planet must contemplate the day when this planet may no longer be inhabitable. Every man, woman and child lives under a nuclear sword of Damocles, hanging by the slenderest of threads, capable of being cut at any moment by accident or miscalculation or madness."

— John F. Kennedy, early 1960s. Assassinated.

Or put it this way:

"It is a strange desire, to seek power, and to lose liberty; or to seek power over others, and to lose power over a man's self."
— Francis Bacon (1561-1626), British philosopher, essayist, statesman.

189

And this from James Paul Warburg (1896-1969), while speaking before the United States Senate, February 17, 1950. He is the son of Paul Moritz Warburg, nephew of Felix Warburg and of Jacob Schiff, both of Kuhn, Loeb & Co. which poured millions into the Russian Revolution through James' brother Max, banker to the German government:

"We shall have World Government, whether or not we like it. The only question is whether World Government will be achieved by conquest or consent."

A voice of the (Un)Illuminati perhaps?

The framers of the U.S. Constitution feared if their country 'fell prey' to Central Banking, that they would lose power over their own ability to rule. It seems President Wilson recognized his own folly within three years of passing legislation that created the Federal Reserve:

"I have unwittingly ruined my country. A great industrial nation is controlled by its system of credit. Our system of credit is concentrated. The growth of the nation, therefore, and all our activities are in the hands of a few men. We have come to be one of the worst ruled, **one of the most completely controlled and dominated governments in the civilized world - no longer a government by free opinion, no longer a government by conviction and the vote of the majority, but the government by the opinion and duress of small groups of dominated men."** (My emphasis.)

Controlled and dominated – and that's the U.S. government! And that was in 1913! Who on earth is running the USA, (and the UK and Europe for that matter) NOW......

Bonuses, anyone....?

WDC's – World Domination Cults:

There have been dominators and would-be dominators in every recorded age. In the past it was soldier-warrior-killer-emperors and then religions and now today it is the mega rich, the so-called 'illuminati'. One of the world experts on them is David Icke and you can read him on www.davidicke.com and in his many books. Another is Ian R Crane: www.ianrcrane.co.uk

A time of worldwide openhearted human loving co-operation eludes humanity although there are intimations in old stone tablets and texts (See Barbara G. Walker – WEMS) that such an age may well have existed in the mists of long ago. At the present time there is quite a wake-up going on in many individuals as the ancient wisdoms spread in parallel with the realization that we are currently on an unsustainable road to self-destruction. We have a giant challenge and we know that us humans grow when we have to – crisis births the new opportunity. Let all who are awake put energy behind con-structive change towards a future that we would really like our children to inherit. The next revolution must to come from the grass-roots, it cannot be imposed.

In the words of Keisha – Little Grandmother.

"This is the "death or the end" the Mayans speak about – the death of our planet as we know it. We as human beings have a choice to make with only two options. One, we continue on as we are, blind children constantly gutting Mother Earth for all she is worth, taking without replenishing, using without thanking, pollut-ing the air and the soil, the animals and the plants, killing, raping, abusing, neglecting and torturing each other and Mother Earth, ensuring our death. Or option number two, we witness our mistakes as human beings and come together as one people to start taking

responsibility for our actions. We once again learn the wisdom of the past, the truths that have been lost for so long and act on them."

By the way – the word 'apocalypse' – means 'to unveil, to reveal'.

It does not mean the end of the world.

Chapter 13
Trinities: The balance of spirituality and the imbalance of male-monotheist religion

"Polarity is the loom on which reality is strung." Mayan Oracle

When you went to church (assuming you did), did you just accept the Trinity and pray to it without thinking or did you ever think – *"Hey wait a minute, there's something missing here?"*

Did you ever wonder how come it is all male? Where is the feminine? Where is the balance?

Most spiritual teachings express the godhead as a trinity of:

1. All-That-Is

2. The Feminine

3. The Masculine

Or as expressed in the Far East:

1. The All

2. The Yin

3. The Yang

In essence, all ancient trinities show the Ultimate Creator as All-Potential which became All Manifestation in its two polarities, Feminine and Masculine / Yin and Yang.

Native American cosmology expresses it as:

1. Great Spirit / Great Mystery. (unknowable, unlimited.)

2. Great Grandmother Wakan. (All that is feminine.)

3. Great Grandfather Ssquan. (All that is masculine.)

Our Pagan ancestors likewise saw Creation as a trinity of balance. However, when we get to Christianity, an extraordinary difference occurred. The commonly accepted trinity is:

1. God the Father. (masculine.)

2. God the Son. (masculine.)

3. God the Holy Ghost. (non-gender.)

What happened to the feminine?

"Whatever the economic, political and religious reasons – and make no mistake our religions, from Judaism to Christianity and Islam have contributed massively to (the horrendous treatment of women) – it is important to understand that the way 'half of humanity' is regarded and treated is an indicator of the low worth placed on the feminine within human societies. The implications of this are at the best destructive and at the worst threaten our very existence. Human kind – or better MANkind - has lost the most basic, natural understanding that the feminine, as a principle, is as important as the masculine to create a sustainable whole. The life giving, life preserving, the nurturing, the emotional, the compassionate, the sharing, the deep, the yin has been systematically neglected, belittled, bashed, humiliated, mutilated, tortured, hunted and killed by the male principle that has taken over our thinking and behaving on every level in Society."
Christa Mackinnon, 2010.

And from Keisha Crowther (Little Grandmother):

"We cannot heal the Earth until we heal ourselves, and the biggest wounds we carry as human beings are those buried deep within our masculine and the feminine beings. These two energies have been so out of balance for so long, that it is impossible not to see the damage created by this imbalance in almost every living human on the globe. The imbalance is so great that without rebalancing and healing, we human beings simply will not be able to survive, nor will our planet".

Some recent Stats:

Women perform 66% of the world's work

Produce 50% of the food.

Earn 10% of the income

Own 1% of the property.

Equality is something we do not even scratch the surface of.

We all know that human creation takes one man and one woman, one masculine energy and one feminine energy. Not even the most dedicated same-sex couples have ever managed to create offspring. So how come we expect 'God' to do it? It is completely against everything that we know and everything that is natural!

Now when a culture holds as sacred a Trinity that is all masculine, it indicates that the feminine energy has been seriously demoted, if not virtually deleted, from any place of equality and power.

So just look at what we have done to the primal feminine energy – EVE, GAIA, Our Mother, the Earth. Is it any wonder that, as a culture, we show her no respect. We pollute her, desecrate her, use up her resources carelessly, throw our trash on her, rape her. It is as if the son has usurped the mother in the family trinity and the mother is now pushed aside and reduced to mere servant or even slave.

It is time for a radical solution and there is one:

It is time for Christian religions to take a great step forward, face this gigantic error and correct this imbalance by bringing the feminine back into the Trinity:

> God the Holy Ghost/Holy Spirit
>
> God the Father
>
> God the Mother

Every Sunday, thousands of people still go to churches and worship at this trough of 100% imbalance. What a monumental difference it would make if this were to change. Our Mother is suffering from our lack of love for her, from our collective lack of care for her. Our religious leaders focus on the idea of 'saving souls' but if they do not help in saving our Mother the Earth, there will be no souls to 'save.' The most important issue right now is ecology of the Earth. The other most important issue is ecology of the human being who also requires a proper balance of feminine and masculine.

Perhaps the Church of England, which is ahead in many ways such as promoting women priests and bishops and accepting the role of gay people, could take the lead, blaze a trail, change the Trinity and pave the way towards balance in religion between feminine and masculine. A healthy thought for the Archbishop.

Here is the Hindu concept of Trinity:

Brahman ('Creator' God) *is* Creation. The cosmos is not so much a creation, but more an emanation from Brahma, the Ultimate Creator.

All humans, animals, gods, and even objects, are One-Divine-Being. The soul of each person is thus Brahman, the entirety of creation, and every animal or stone or star is an aspect of Brahman.

This may be a difficult concept to comprehend if you are accustomed to thinking of God as a separate chap in a separate place but it is the comprehension of this very idea that is central to spiritual human life. It is the central understanding of all the indigenous spiritual paths of humans of planet Earth.

The multiplicity that hides the cosmos' unity the Hindus call Maya, the ordinary reality that we humans perceive with our senses every day. The overcoming of Maya to perceive True Reality (Brahman) constitutes 'The Task' in Hinduism. You and God are One but the challenge is to realize it deep within.

So, for Hinduism, there may be millions of gods. However, these gods are not God-God, they cannot create stars, or planets, or plants or animals – or humans. "Brahman" is The One Absolute, the Ultimate God.

Though believed by many to be a polytheistic religion, the basis of Hinduism is the belief in the unity of everything. This totality – Brahman - is the Absolute, the Supreme Being, the Ultimate Reality, the Divine. The purpose of life is to realize that we are part of God. For most Hindus, this God is not a person but a force, an energy.

All the so-called pantheistic religions I have studied hold, under the Pantheon, this same concept of Oneness, Unity,

Absolute, Single, Beingness. This Unity we can call Creator is expressed in and through Creation. There is no separation. Creator is everywhere in Creation. In the ancient animist/ shamanist spiritual ways, the cosmos is seen as a Unity and its expression is nature. This Native American medicine wheel, known as the Earth Count, tells of this understanding of Creation poetically:

The Earth Count:

In the beginning was the Great Round, the Zero, the No-Thing which is the potential of All Things, the Womb of all Life that births All Existence. All the Children of Creation are designed in the Zero and from the Zero come forth into manifestation.

The Zero is the Marriage of All-That-Is-Feminine – Great Grandmother Wakan – and All-That-Is-Masculine – Great Grandfather Ssquan, the Lightning bolt who potentizes the zero of potential into manifestation.

Creation, for us, began when Great Grandmother Wakan and Great Grandfather Ssquan made Love and gave birth to their first born, Grandfather Sun.

Grandfather Sun is given the number One. He rises in the East, so we place him on the Medicine Wheel in the Easterly Direction.

Great Grandfather and Great Grandmother made love a second time and gave birth to Grandmother Earth. Grandmother is given the number Two, and we place her opposite the Sun on the West of the Wheel.

Then Grandfather Sun and Grandmother Earth made love and they gave birth to their first born, the Kingdom of Plants. The plants thrive in the summer and they depend on water so we place them in the South direction of the Wheel. (It is a northern hemisphere teaching) Their number is Three, which is the sum of One and Two.

Grandmother and Grandfather made love again and gave birth to their second born, the Kingdom of Animals. The animals breathe the air and we place them on the North of the wheel. Their number is Four, which is the sum of One and Two plus One.

Grandmother and Grandfather made love a third time and gave birth to their third born, the Kingdom of Humans. The place of the Humans is in the Centre of the Wheel but towards the South because Humans are as yet children of the Cosmos. We are the one kingdom that is still incomplete and we are still learning who we are. Our number is Five.

Number six is our ancestors and our history. Six is the number of all directions: East, West, South, North, Above and Below. Six is placed in the Southeast direction between fire and water.

Seven is the number of the six directions plus the power of Light (One). It is the 'Dream' of Creation. In the energy of the Dream, there is no time and no matter, there is just the 'Dream of Life'. The 'Dream' is placed on the Wheel in the Southwest, between Earth and Water.

Eight is the number of cycles and circles, pattern and repetition, physical laws. It is the 'form' of the 'dream.' Eight is the number for the Natural Law of the Universe, for Karma – the power of action-brings-reaction – which maintains balance and harmony in all things. Eight is placed in the Northwest between earth and air.

Nine is the number for Movement and Change. It is the number for Sister Moon who moves the tides and winds of Earth, and moves the tidal waves of blood within all living beings who have hearts and the power of movement. Nine is placed Northeast between air and fire.

Ten is the number for Pure Intellect and Measure of all material things. It is the power of Movement and Change (9) plus the Light (1). Ten is the number for our Spirit-Twin or Higher-Self. The ten is placed to the north of the centre of the wheel.

(See *LightningBolt* by Hyemeyohsts Storm and *The View Through The Medicine Wheel* by Leo Rutherford. Also teachings of Harley Swiftdeer: www.dtmms.org)

Earth my body, Water my blood

Air my breath and Fire my spirit

THE EARTH COUNT

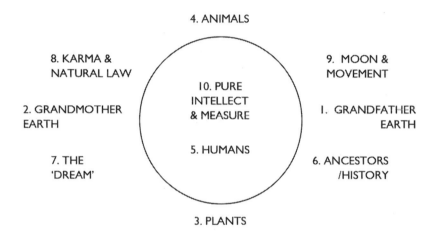

4. ANIMALS

8. KARMA & NATURAL LAW

9. MOON & MOVEMENT

10. PURE INTELLECT & MEASURE

2. GRANDMOTHER EARTH

1. GRANDFATHER EARTH

5. HUMANS

7. THE 'DREAM'

6. ANCESTORS /HISTORY

3. PLANTS

This is a small part of a much bigger teaching of the powers of the Universe and how they interact to create the reality we experience. Like all pre-patriarchal religion, they show that All comes from Oneness, Unity.

There is no separation.

'God' means Creator-Creation

Judaism, Christianity, Islam, all of the Abrahamic male-monotheist religions of the last maybe 6,000 or so years, have taken a disastrous turn away from ancient knowledge. They have made a separation of their 'God' from Creation so He (not she, no balance of forces, just masculine only, thank you) has become Big-Daddy-in-the-Sky, the 'God-Chap'. A symbol for adults who don't want to grow up and take responsibility for themselves and for the earth, but want a 'God' to give them rights to dominate and to steal from other cultures with other spiritual ways. And they want this 'God-Chap' to give them an easy and effortless passage to 'heaven'. (eg: 'The 'Rapture' as described in the last chapter.)

Here is a Native American's feelings about the Christian God-Chap brought by the European invaders of his land:

"I do not want your god.
You say the devil is in the wilderness,
But the greatest peace I have ever known is with the sun shining bright,
The wind blowing on my burned face,
Or the moon shining like the sun on a solstice

You believe the annihilation of my ancestors is divinely authorized.
Even your religious coercions today are still cultural genocide,
As you make darkness bow its head in shame for the choices you make

I do not want your god.
Every time you say your Devil's name he comes and dances
Though you say he's "under your feet."
It's your Devil, you keep him

I do not want your god.
And while your Religious Fascism killed my clan,
Who knows not who they are –
I forgive you, the white man,
But I'll never forget

I do not want your god.
I may not know where the bones of my ancestors are,
Whose culture your Religious Fascism murdered -
But they breath through me,
I know who I am.
I do not need your god to be free.
I am free of hate,
I am free of fear,
And all I see with your god is hate and fear

I do not want your god."

And then there's this thing about saviors: –

"One of the most common and recurring religious themes is
that humanity will be saved and brought to its next stage of evolution through the appearance of a yet another great prophet or
world teacher. In Christianity, Christ will come again. In Buddhism,
the Maitreya Buddha will incarnate. In Judaism, the Messiah.
In Islam, the Imam Mahdi. And across the new age movement,
there are all kinds of prophesies about new gurus, avatars and
interventions.

I am open to all these ideas – I always welcome help! – but to
be honest I am also suspicious of them. These prophecies suggest
that humanity is dependent on outside intervention and that we
cannot make it by ourselves. Maybe so, but I have another experience. I know the world is full of selfishness and suffering, but over
and over again I see people growing and transforming. Especially in
crises and challenges I see people developing. I therefore have faith
in our species to achieve spiritual maturity and fulfillment based in
our own efforts.

So I prefer another idea and prophesy, which is that humanity
as a whole is the new saviour and that collectively we are the new
Messiah. Or to put it in another language, the Christ consciousness,

the Buddha consciousness, the Gaia consciousness, will not be manifest through just one single person, but **will manifest through many of us. It will be a group event."** (My emphasis added) From writer/teacher William Bloom.

Yes and yes again! It is up to us. <u>We</u> make the changes. We need to grow up and stop expecting someone else to do it for us. We are responsible – and if we are not, it is for us to learn to be – and soon! That itself is part of the change.

Cauldron of Changes, Feather on the bone,

 Arc of eternity, Hole in the stone.

  We are the old people, We are the new people,

  We are the same people, <u>Wiser than before</u>.....

Let us make it so!

Chapter 14
Transformation – on becoming
one's own mystic

Here are some general thoughts as to where one might and might not look for guidance and wisdom:

- For spiritual understanding – avoid most churches and don't believe their Bibles.

- For true information – avoid corporately 'owned' media

- For real healthy food with less pesticide concentrations – avoid many of the usual supermarkets. Buy organic if you can.

- For good health – seek 'alternative' whole person medicine first and go to allopathic doctors for emergencies, accidents etc.

- For history – avoid official HIS-story and seek underground suppressed knowledge. Especially HER-story.

- For self-understanding – avoid consensus education and psychiatry and seek the ancient knowledge of the shamans and wise people of the earth-based cultures.

Who are we? The God-Man myth:

Let us look again at this story as it originally was – a teaching story for all of us – the Son of God story as an eternal myth.

It is the *Sun* of God, personalized. It is a guide for all people, 'His' life is your life in potential, 'His' story is a metaphor for your story as the events in 'His' mythological life happen in yours. Remember, a myth is something that is always true but never necessarily happened. The challenges 'He' faces in 'His' story are the same archetypal ones you face in your life.

The journey has been described in many ways by many cultures and called by many names: The Jesus Story as understood by the Original Gnostic Christians; the Perennial Philosophy; the Search for the Holy Grail; the Buddha's search for enlightenment; the Arthurian legends; the Journey of Osiris/Dionysus; the Journey around the Medicine Wheel of life; the Journey into the Mind of God; and so on. Here, as I have come to understand it, is the essence of the God-(Wo) Man's Journey:

We are all born away from our home which is the spirit world. We are born to parents who created our body-vehicle but not our spirit. They are not our real parents who are (quite literally) Father Sun (or Father Sky) and Mother Earth (Virgin Mare). Our birth is supported by spirit guides / 'angels' (messengers) who assist our spirit in our early years to adapt to the body-vehicle and its environment. They assist but they do not interfere. This is our journey and our experience.

At around the age of twelve we tend to challenge the status quo. We go through puberty, we manifest our 'weapons of mass creation' becoming sexual beings, and we start to take on responsibility for our self and to take our place in society. We seek a job or vocation and we begin to contribute to the collective and earn our own living. Most create a family and make a 'giveaway' to their children for the future.

We are tempted by the counter force, struggle with all the challenges of human life, and we have to make up our own mind whether we live with integrity or not and to what extent. We are challenged by the 'Cross', the limiting and restricting powers of the Four Directions, the powers of Earth, Air, Water and Fire which in us are the Body, Mind, Emotions and Life force.

We are challenged ultimately to die to our ego-separateness and to be 'reborn' in conscious Oneness with God-Spirit-Universe-Creation, living as part of the Great Unity of All-Things. Each one of us is the 'Christ-upon-the-Cross' of matter and we are spirit 'crucified' = constricted within the limitations of the body and the third dimensional world of gross matter.

Our task to achieve maturity is to die to our egotism; to get down off the cross of limitation; to REAL-ize that we are part of the energy source that creates the Universe; to consciously become Masters of our own Self, Co-Creators of our own Destiny and participants in the Evolution of All-That-Is.

In other words, to become our own mystics.

Shamanic mystical visionary ecstasy is the path to connection with the Goddess / God of the Earth and All-That-Is, and is the gateway to the delightful, amazing and magical experience of the universe as energy. Touching the *mysterium tremendum,* the mystic state of ex-stasis, outside of the normal boundaries that control, limit and restrict our consciousness, this is the threshold to ecstasy.

The monkey mind has shut up, the inner dialogue is switched off, the past and future cease all relevance and there is just existence now in all its glory. In this wordless, conceptless realm of full emptiness, we touch 'God', The Source, The Essence, and we feel pure joy.

This is way beyond 'faith' which turns out to be a useful concept to keep us going on through the challenges of life. It shows us that beliefs are generally irrelevant and often ridiculous constructs. We touch the bottom line of pure being and there is nothing to be thought, believed, assumed; nothing to be said, nothing to be done and no one to do it – there is no-thing! Existence just Is. Timeless – Glorious!

Experience of this state gives us glimpses of the intrinsic unity of the Universe and of ourselves as integral; the sublime majesty of our Universe revealed.

Inevitably we come back to ordinary reality, to duality, but however short the magic moment, our soul is fed and we carry on with our daily lives, conscious from a different place inside. We have glimpsed the multi-dimensional and know that the ordinary world is just one part of what is.

Life is a movement from babyhood to elderhood in which we learn to grow up and take full responsibility for ourselves, our feelings and our actions. We are challenged to learn to love all that is just the way it is in spite of all the imperfections. And to realize fully we are each part of it and not separate.

That means when we love All-That-Is, we are loving our own Self. And when we hate All-That-Is, we are hating our own Self.

Teacher Byron Katie has this to say:

"The apparent craziness of the world, like everything else, is a gift we can use to set our minds free. Any stressful thought you have about the planet, for example, or about life and death, shows you where you're stuck, where your energy is being exhausted as a result of not fully meeting life as it is, without conditions. You can't free yourself by finding a so-called 'enlightened' state outside your own mind. When you question what you believe, you eventually come to see you're the enlightenment you've been seeking. Until you can love what is-everything, including the apparent violence and craziness — you're separate from the world, and you'll see it as dangerous and frightening. I invite everyone to put their fearful thoughts on paper, to do The Work — question their stressful, fearful thoughts,

and set themselves free. When the mind is not at war with itself, it is free, free to love, free to serve others and free to create what is beautiful."

When we can love our-self then we can love all other. The solution is us. As the Hopis say – "We are the people we have been waiting for."

Why are we here?

Our mission in life as human beings seen through the lens of Native American culture:

"Every life form has one common mission as well as their individual ones. Each life-form is created to learn to be an equal contributor to the beauty of the whole. The purpose of the common mission is to discover who you are, why you are here, what talents you can use to assist the whole, and how you are going to go about it. The mission of discovery is the Sacred Path of Beauty that allows every living creature to express uniqueness in a way that exemplifies harmony and truth

The human race is the only one of All Our Relations that has lost the inner-knowing about its purpose. The two-leggeds have been given much assistance by Great Mystery since they must answer the questions of the common mission before understanding the value of their individual missions." – Jamie Sams. Sacred Path.

Life is not a scientific accident or a solo program of a crazy disconnected Universe, it is a purposeful journey of exploration and learning. We have both common purpose and individual purpose. We are not alone, we are part of All-That-Is and we are wanted, we are necessary and we are loved. We have our challenges to overcome and our missions to fulfill.

At this time we are on the cusp of ages, moving from the Age of Pisces to the Age of Aquarius. We have had two thousand years or more of believing what we're told, of denying our own connection to Mother Earth and Father Sky, of being made malleable, controllable, disconnected, of becoming lost souls. It is time for soul retrieval on a global scale. It is time to find the mystic within, the shaman within, to return to individual connection with the great powers, to the path that leads to self-mastery, self-honor and self- love. Then we will once again be able to live in balance and harmony and to walk the good true road on planet earth.

Here is a very important piece of ancient shamans' wisdom:

Where are we going? Imagination comes before reality:

It is important to remember this truth. For example: your house was a thought before it was built. It was somebody's 'dream', then the architect came and made plans on paper, the quantity surveyor calculated the materials required and so on. Only finally did the builders come and put it all together. What we experience as 'reality' is the final step in the process of creating /thinking / 'dreaming'!

When I talk of imagination, I think of 'The Mage', of 'magic'. This is where all creativity starts, all change starts.

When we desire to manifest something in the external world we first go inside, think about it and 'dream' it. The weather shaman communicates with the 'weather spirits', the energies of the wind, the rain, the clouds etc, and 'dreams' the weather desired on, around and in him/her self. The message is sent through feeling, emotion (energy-motion). We are part of all that is around us. There is no separation. Hence we influence everything and everything influences us.

"All human ideas are birthed from the spirit inside the human body, are fed to the brain, and then acted upon through the will of the total being. All ideas in Creation come from the Great Mystery, are gathered by Great Spirit, and then are used to feed the rest of Creation. Jamie Sams. Sacred Path.

However, we need to watch out for the internal saboteur whose voice tells us such things as we don't deserve, we are never going to succeed, we are not worthy and so on. Usually old parental, teacher, boss voices of way back who also suffered from the same voices handed down to them.

We need to circumvent any such negativity by humoring it, allowing it to run but giving it no energy, while holding steadfastly onto the dream we seek to create. And then we put our clear intent into the stream of the unfolding 'I-The-Mage –A-Nation' and hold it firm as already manifested in spirit. Then we let go and wait until the outcome is manifest into ordinary reality.

There is a caveat to that seemingly nice and easy process. It tends not to work for ego desires or ego inflation. It works to help others, to create something to help the collective, but not for selfish desires. Remember, the ultimate dreamer is The Source – Creator-God – and we live in Creator's Dream. We are part of, not a solo entity, so desires to get more at the expense of others gums up the process. We are here to contribute to the greater good, not to take from it just for our egoic satisfaction. (There has been some seriously misguided teaching circulated about this in recent years.)

Duality, opposites, contrast:

Many people ask, "How can a Loving-God countenance all the suffering in the world?" But the world is set up on the basis of opposites, of duality. How can you describe 'good' except in terms of 'bad'? How can you know love without knowing betrayal, abandonment and all that is not loving? How can any-one be a hero or heroine without a villain to challenge? Without both 'good' and 'bad,' there is no story, no opportunity, no development. The Chinese have it right as their word for 'opportunity' is the same as their word for 'crisis.' Both go together.

Have you read the wonderful stories of Harry Potter and the world of Wizards? How much fun would those stories be without the fantastically evil, total egotist villain, Lord Voldemort? It is the challenge of duality that makes the stories hum, the challenge of good vs evil which we can translate as the challenge between the desire to do good for all vs the desire to serve self at the expense of other. Harry grows through the challenges from the dark villians. This is a crux in life for each of us.

We live between opposites. If there was no negative energy, then there would be no positive either. Chocolate is fabulous but too much will kill you. Love is wonderful but too much can make you feel suffocated. Freedom is great but without any control it becomes chaos. Control is needed but too much is stultifying. This is our realm of learning and there are no absolutes. The perfected man is a myth, he cannot be literal because that would be contrary to nature. The Yin is never completely yin and the Yang is never completely yang. That is how God/Spirit/Creator set it up.

This world exists in paradox:

The Universe lives in a state of dynamic disequilibrium. DIS-equilibrium. Slight, subtle, but nevertheless there. Phi is the Golden Mean or Fibonacci Ratio after the 16th century mathematician Leonardo de Pisa, a very important ratio that occurs in nature in an amazing variety of situations. It is calculated by adding the last number to the present number to get the next one: i.e., 1, 1, 2, 3, 5, 8, 13, 21, 34, 55, etc. When you boil

that down to a ratio, it is a ratio that never resolves. 1.618....
forever

Then there is Pi, the ratio of the diameter of a circle to the
circumference. 3.1418..... That, too, never resolves.

Just suppose these numbers did resolve and the yin did
become totally yin and the yang totally yang, what then?

Well, everything would reach equilibrium. How wonderful
you might think. Now we can all stop worrying and have a nice
cup of tea. Or something stronger, perhaps. Ahh, but that in
itself will recreate disequilibrium!

No, the point is that everything would stop moving and
changing. Stop moving, become static, the same, stuck, no
growth, no energy, no development, no change, no progression,
no uncertainly, no freedom, no point. And that means no life.

The Universe must exist in dis-equilibrium, in perfect
imperfection, in order to exist as an ongoing creation. What is
actually so amazing is that the illusion of existence we experience is so consistent! That the necessary state of dis-equilibrium is so subtle as to be virtually unapparent.

This from writer Tom Robbins:

*"Well, it's about time we came to terms with the paradoxical
nature of the universe. The great struggle in life is not between good
and evil, which are both relative terms, but between the desire for
certainty and the desire for freedom. Freedom and certainty cannot
equally coexist. The more you have of one, the less you have of the
other. And certainty is merely an illusionary product of fear.*

*On perhaps an even wider scale, the dichotomy is between
the Big Lie and the Big Joke. If you don't want to be controlled and
manipulated by the Big Lie – as perpetrated by all of our institutions: governmental, corporate, academic, social and religious – then
your only choice is to recognize and embrace the Big Joke."*

Or put it this way –

"Since things neither exist nor do not exist,

Are neither real nor unreal,

Are utterly beyond adopting and rejecting –

One might as well burst out laughing."

Tibetan Nyingmapa master - Longchenpa Rabjampa - C14th.

Now he REALLY knew what he was talking about!

The Mayans say: *"In Lakech,"* meaning, *"I am another yourself, you are another myself."* We are all One. What we do to others, we do to aspects of our self. The answer to human life is the recognition deep inside that All-Is-One, that 'God' is The-Creation-We-Live-In-As-Part-Of.

"The deepest level of truth uncovered by science and by philosophy is the fundamental truth of The Unity. At that deepest subnuclear level of our reality, you and I are literally one." John Hagelin PhD. Quantum physicist, from *The Little Book of Bleeps*

And in the words of Albert Einstein:

"A human being is part of the whole called by us Universe, a part limited in time and space. He experiences himself, his thoughts and feelings as something separated from the rest, a kind of optical delusion of his consciousness. This delusion is a kind of prison for us, restricting us to our personal desires and to affection for a few persons nearest to us. Our task must be to free ourselves from this prison by widening our circle of compassion to embrace all living creatures and the whole of nature and its beauty."

And what is Knowledge:… *"To know that we know what we know, and to know that we do not know what we do not know, that is true knowledge."* — Copernicus.

"Knowing others is intelligence; knowing yourself is true wisdom. Mastering others is strength; mastering yourself is true power." ~ Lao-Tzu.

We are at a crucial point in our evolution here on Planet Earth and we have mega big and important choices to make which will determine our future:

Community

We need to move toward replacing competition with co-operation, separated living in tiny units to community living where we can mutually support each other more easily, where we can share what is available and consume considerably less per capita. We need to remember we are all part of one whole. We will survive by cooperation and sharing.

Givers Not Takers

We in the 'developed' world need to live like 'Givers' not 'Takers'; to think many generations ahead; to consider the welfare of other humans all over the world; the welfare of other kingdoms of the planet; to recognize we are just one species that lives here and while it is our home, it is not 'our' planet. To accept that we are responsible for the future we create through our actions.

God, the Real-One that is All-That-Is, has (definitely, maybe!) set up this planetary existence as a challenging, learning place for the many aspects of Him/Her/Itself that inhabit it. We don't and can't know all the whys and wherefores but we can speculate. Some of our ancestors called God the 'Great Mystery' and that surely describes existence well. Each of us is a part of it and is here to learn and grow and develop within it. No one can die for your 'sins', your life problems and challenges, and no amount of 'belief' will save you from reaping the rewards of how you live your life. This is often called 'karma', meaning the life lessons we are here to learn.

We live in a hall of mirrors and life is forever reflecting our-self to Our-Self. The challenge is to stop, listen, see and feel what is being reflected. That pushes us towards personal evolvement which is what we are here for. How does THE WHOLE (God) grow and develop?

One way is through us!

We are conscious aspects of Great Mystery, experiencing Itself from within. As in their different ways are the animals, the birds, the plants, the insects, the planets, the suns – everything in its own way lives and experiences it's Self as a form of life.

The Great Mystery experiences all that is within Its Body which is All the Universes.

How much better to try to understand each other, to co-operate first before we compete, to live together in harmony rather than try to exterminate each other, to stop believing fundamentalist, literalist, religio-corporate brainwash. We're going to have to anyway because if we don't and we set off our WMD toys, there won't be much left of anyone or for anyone.

The human race at the moment is a bit like a bunch of paranoid schizophrenics who are so determined they are right and so terrified of others with different skins, ideas and beliefs, that they think they are all out to get him, so he seeks to exterminate them first, till he is the last living being, safe, and all alone.

Yes, alone is safe! But that was the condition of Great-Mystery prior to Creation! Great-Spirit-Creator-God was alone – which is also ALL-ONE. And Great-Spirit chose to create a matrix of apparent reality to play in so as to learn to co-operate and to love and to grow. Planet Earth is God's Growth Group! With God as All the Participants!

It's a joke, folks, a big fat Cosmic Joke, and it's calling us to WAKE UP!

Last Word:

Please don't be-lie-ve a word of this book! Let my words affect you, stimulate you, catalyze you to think and seek for yourself. But no more 'being-in-the-lie'. Trust only your own experience, your own truth, your own inner knowing. It's the only truth you've got and will ever have

Our myths and legends have been skewed and screwed to give a toxic foundation to our society which is reflected in the dire toxic effects we are having on Planet Earth. We have been misled to look at life in terms of the Newtonian / computerised way of *either–or* (the 'Binary Con') rather than the Quantum understanding of *both–and*. It is time to transform our way of thinking and being, to embrace the world as a quantum phenomenon, an energy phenomenon, just as the shamans have maintained through millennia.

We have been taught to worship at the altar of a false all-masculine 'God-Chap' and it's time to move on from 'him' and transform ourselves and how we live. We have lost our sense of belonging to the earth, of it being our home, and we have been conned into looking at it and its kingdoms as objects.

We have become what we believed. We believed in a male-dominator war-god and became war-like seekers of domination – and it is time we change – and soon.

Many of the old cultures have legends that say this is the third, fourth or even fifth world and suggest that previous humanities have reached this place in evolution and a mass extinction has occurred. We can see all around us the potential for this happening again. It seems that Creation (God) has set Itself-In-Us a giant task to get past this enormous challenge. That means to wake up, to grow up, to come out of the lies, face ourselves, take responsibility for our actions and the results of those actions and to look after each other in the deep knowledge that we are ultimately One.

It is possible for us to create a 'new world' for the benefit of everyone. Each of us can take steps to manifest our spiritually-connected / earth-connected Mystic-Self instead of living as the competitive, separate, warring, egotistical human fool.

Many of us received a demolition job on our self worth during childhood and adolescence because most of our parents and teachers received the same in their time and knew no different. It has come down many European/Middle Eastern ancestral lines for centuries since the terrible days of the Inquisition, and before then too. Most of us have grown up with cockeyed mythologies and been force fed beliefs and guilt.

It is now time to challenge these toxic beliefs and manifest the best in us, the God-Wo/Man within. To help the human world towards recognition of the ecological catastrophe on our doorstep and the realization of the urgent need for sustainable living; to awaken to the madness of war; to embrace a loving, compassionate, co-operative, peaceful path of life and a 'God' to suit; to become part of the solution; to recognize we are ultimately just One Being and that whatever we are doing, we are doing to Our-Self.

"Make the most of yourself, for that is all there is of you" –
Ralph Waldo Emerson.

And here's a great thought to close with:

*"There comes a time when you have to stand up and shout:
This is me damn it! I look the way I look, think the way I think, feel
the way I feel, love the way I love! I am a whole complex package.
Take me... or leave me. Accept me - or walk away! Do not try to
make me feel like less of a person just because I don't fit your idea
of who I should be and don't try to change me to fit your mold. If I
need to change, I alone will make that decision.*

*When you are strong enough to love yourself 100%, good and
bad - you will be amazed at the opportunities that life presents
you."* ~ Stacey Charter.

Right on!

Don't be 'sheeple'; strut your stuff and be true to yourself!

Don't be believers; be a finder-out, get informed.

Don't be followers; become your own mystic.

Remember – you are spirit in a body; you are immortal,
just the outer body is born here and dies; what you experience while in body is your lessons and your learning is through
dealing with the challenges life brings you. You, as spirit, are
eternal; time is part of this reality but not of eternity.

Right now you are in the midst of your Earth-Walk so
which life would you rather help to create here? Who of

your possible selves would you rather grow into and live as? What future do you wish for your children? What do you seek to leave behind as your contribution to human life on the earth?

Time to wake up

To act for the good of all

For the long term future of Planet Earth

And all her inhabitants

Who knows – one day you may want to take on another body and come back!

SOURCES (With Thanks) and REFERENCES.

THE JESUS MYSTERIES by Timothy Freke and Peter Gandy. Harper Collins / Thorsons 1999. Republished by Element 2003

JESUS AND THE (LOST) GODDESS by same authors. Harper Collins / Thorsons 2001.

THE LAUGHING JESUS – RELIGIOUS LIES AND GNOSTIC WISDOM by same authors. Harmony Books (Random House) 2005.

THE CHRIST CONSPIRACY – The greatest story ever sold. By Acharys S. 1999. Adventures Unlimited Press, 1999.

THE BOOK YOUR CHURCH DOESN'T WANT YOU TO READ. Edited by Tim C. Leedom. Kendall / Hunt Publishing Co, Iowa, USA. 1993

THE DARK SIDE OF CHRISTIAN HISTORY. By Helen Ellerbe. Published By Morningstar And Lark, USA. 1995. Seventh printing 2004.

THE WOMAN'S ENCYCLOPEDIA OF MYTHS AND SECRETS by Barbara G Walker, Harper, San Francisco, 1983.

THE GENIUS OF THE FEW by Christian and Barbara Joy O'Brien. Duanthus Publishing, Pool House, Kemble, Cirencester, England GL7 6AD, 1999.

KING JESUS: FROM KAM (EGYPT) TO CAMELOT: King Jesus of Judaea, by Ralph Ellis (Paperback - 15 Jun 2008)

THE BIBLE FRAUD: An Untold Story of Jesus Christ by Tony Bushby (Perfect Paperback - 2001)

THE LAST HOURS OF ANCIENT SUNLIGHT by Thom Hartmann. Hodder and Stoughton 1998.

CARE OF THE SOUL by Thomas Moore. Piatkus 1992.

LIGHTNINGBOLT by Hyemeyohsts Storm. Ballantine 1994.

METAPHYSICAL BIBLE DICTIONARY. Unity School of Christianity, Unity Village, Mo, USA

BEFORE GOD THE FATHER by Mary Daly. Beacon Press, Boston 1973.

NEMU'S END —History, Psychology and Poetry of the Apocalypse by Reverend Nemu. Psychedelic Press, UK 2009

THE SACRED PATH CARDS by Jamie Sams. HarperSan Francisco 1990.

THE CHALICE AND THE BLADE by Riane Eisler

ROGUE NATION by Vernon Coleman. Blue Books 2003

CHRISTIANITY AS MYSTICAL FACT by Rudolph Steiner. Anthroposophic Press 1972.

THE GOD DELUSION by Richard Dawkins. 2006. Black swan.

HOW JESUS BECAME CHRISTIAN by Barrie Wilson. Orion Books 2008

SINNERS IN THE HANDS OF AN ANGRY GOD — Jonathan Edwards (Boston, 1742)

CHRISTIANITY, AN ANCIENT EGYPTIAN RELIGION by Ahmed Osman

DECEPTIONS AND MYTHS OF THE BIBLE by Lloyd Graham (2000)

BOUDICA: DREAMING THE EAGLE (Series of four) by Manda Scott. Bantam Press 2003-7

CHILDREN AT RISK: THE BATTLE FOR THE HEARTS AND MINDS OF OUR KIDS. By James Dobson. World Publishing, 1990.

SOURCES (With Thanks) and REFERENCES.

THE LITTLE BOOK OF BLEEPS. Includes writing by John Hagelin PhD. (Revolver Books, 2004)

VACCINATION IS NOT IMMUNIZATION by Dr Tim O'Shea. 2010

THE TWELFTH PLANET by Zecharia Sitchin. 1976 (And many other books)

STUPID WHITE MEN by Michael Moore. 2001

On Injure-Cation:

THE MAKING OF THEM. by Nick Duffell. Lone Arrow Press, 2000.

THE OLD SCHOOL TIE by Jonathan Gathorne-Hardy. Viking Press, New York.

On female genital mutilation:

WOMEN OF OMDURMAN – Life, love and the cult of virginity. By Anne cloudsley. Ethnographia 1981/3.

DO THEY HEAR YOU WHEN YOU CRY by Fauziya Kassindja (1998)

Blogs.

WILLIAM BLOOM. PhD, http://www.williambloom.com/holismnetwork.php

CHRISTA MACKINNON, BSc,DFC,DITEC,PgDHyp, FBSCH,FBAMH,GHR   http://christamackinnon.blogspot.com

NEIL KRAMER. http://neilkramer.com/

BYRON KATIE. http://www.thework.com

DAVID ICKE   http://www.davidicke.com/

IAN R CRANE   http:// ianrcrane.co.uk

VANDANA SHIVA See - http://www.navdanya.org/

Pamphlets published by SEE SHARP PRESS, USA

www.seesharppress.com (Highly recommended)

AMERICA'S TALIBAN in its own words by David W Irish. 2003

THE HERETICS GUIDE TO THE BIBLE. Ed. Chaz Bufe. 1987

PAGAN CHRISTS by Joseph McCabe. 1999

JUDEO-CHRISTIAN DEGRADATION OF WOMEN. By Joseph McCabe. 1998

Magazines

SACRED HOOP MAGAZINE, Anghorfa, Abercych, Bonbcath, Pembs SA37 0EZ www.sacredhoop.net

NEXUS MAGAZINE, 55 Queens Road, East Grinstead, West Sussex, RH19 1BG, UK

CADUCEUS MAGAZINE, 9 Nine Acres, Midhurst, West Sussex, GU29 9EP, UK

Websites:

www.evilbible.com (A wealth of useful info)

www.becomingachristian.com (unbelievably simplistic)

http://www.jesusneverexisted.com/egypt.htm

http://oror.essortment.com/constantine_rbsr.htm (Info on Emperor Constantine)

http://www.skepticsannotatedbible.com/women/long.html

www.angelfire.com

http://100prophecies.org/christianity.htm

www.religionfacts.com

http://geneva.rutgers.edu/src/christianity/major.html

http://www.catholic.com/library/Birth_Control.asp

http://www.languedoc-france.info/1201_beliefs.htm

SOURCES (With Thanks) and REFERENCES.

http://www.califmall.com/earthstarconsultingcom/aboutHDSarticle54.htm

www.cuttingedge.org

http://www.genesis.net.au/~bible/kjv/genesis/

http://www.dhushara.com/book/diversit/saceve.htm#anchor3147959

http://www.dhushara.com/book/zulu/islamp/nakface/naked.htm#anchor205500

http://home.earthlink.net/~pgwhacker/ChristianOrigins/

http://www.medmalexperts.com/POCM/triumph_over_other_Christianities.htm

Biography: KIESHA CROWTHER, (Little Grandmother), was initiated as shaman at age 30 by her mother's tribe (Sioux/Salish), and has been recognized by the Continental Council of Indigenous Elders as Wisdom Keeper of North America, responsible for guiding the "Tribe of Many Colors."

Made in the USA
Charleston, SC
17 May 2014